D1250161

More Than Baseball

By

Coach

DAVE JORN

© 2022 Dave Jorn. All Rights Reserved

This book or any portion thereof may not be reproduced or used in any manner whatsoever without written permission of the publisher except for the use of brief quotations in a book review.

TABLE OF CONTENTS

DEDICATION

I dedicate this book to everyone I had the chance to coach and the coaches that have been in my life.

Without the players and coaches all of this would not have been possible. It's because of all of you that this book could have even come about. Thanks to all of you who made a dream come true.

And in addition, I wanted to express this additional thought. From the beginning til now there has been many, many people in my life who have impacted it and those that I have had the pleasure of relationship with. Other coaches, early mentors, teachers, players, ministers, family members, etc. I have been Blessed by the Lord to have had all of these different people pour into my development and life. I could write another book to name them all, so please understand when I have not mentioned you in a story or particular phase of my like. There are so many more stories that could have been included in my book. So if I left something out or just plain forgot about, which is very possible for me, let me know and we can include it in another book. In fact, I welcome any stories that you have. Thanks to all that made this book possible.

PS. A special thanks to my very good friend and brother in Christ Ron Harris for prodding me to do this book.

FORWARD

As I look back on my life it's amazing how God orchestrated it! Baseball was always going to be my career path, even though I never realized how much. I never had a plan, post-playing. My focus had always been on playing and making it to the big leagues. Never had a backup plan. So the next step, post-playing, naturally transitioned into coaching.

Amazingly, or better yet through divine blessings, the Lord directed and set up my path in coaching. You see it goes back, at least to 1979, when I let my fire and temper get the best of me. That night, in my manager's office in St. Pete, Florida, I pretty much sealed my fate by having that confrontation with the Cardinals farm director.

But out of that, God arranged my next career path, you see my manager that year in 1979, Sonny Roberto liked and respected me. And it just so happened that he was assigned to manage the double-A team in Little Rock, where I so desperately wanted to progress to. Unbeknown to me at the time, I was to be released out of spring training, but Sonny fought to take me with him to Little Rock on the disabled list, even though I knew I was not injured.

It was there in Little Rock, that I pitched versus the University of Arkansas in a pre-season exhibition game, and next when it came time for me, in my post-playing days, to consider my future. Coaching was my new passion.

Well, Coach Norm Debriyn was one of the people I sent a resume to. He remembered me pitching against them and he hired me. It just so happened his pitching coach just left for another job and the position was open. Definitely God's timing!!

I even got the chance to return to Arkansas in 2002 when Coach Debriyn retired and my friend, Dave Van Horn, got the head coaching job and he offered me the pitching coach job. God's timing and grace once again blessed me. I took the job and it turned out to be the best decision I ever made. The best decision besides accepting Jesus Christ as Lord and Savior of my life!

I write all this to express to you how God can orchestrate our lives. He has blessed me beyond measure! God wanted me here at the U of A. Even though I had my own plans, His was what led to my salvation and my marriage to the most Godly and loving woman any man would ever want. And to the most enjoyable 20 years of coaching and mentoring young boys into men.

PROLOGUE

"There is no failure, except in no longer trying"

- Elbert Hubbard

This book is an accumulation of my experiences through the world of baseball. What started out as a hobby, grew into a passion spanning several decades. As I look back through the years, I feel my experience can serve as a teacher to others, not just for those looking to venture into the world of coaching, but also for those facing challenges on the pathway to achieving their dreams and ambitions.

Everyone has a particular skill and talent which if pursued relentlessly in the face of adversity, can take them to great lengths in this world. My journey has not been easy as you will witness through reading these pages. The only difference between me and those who give up was simply I never gave up.

All of my life I kept asking the same question, "Where did I come from and why me Lord?"

You see, I am the eldest of four sons, and I received all the athletic talent that my other brothers never had or experienced and I was given many opportunities to travel the world, also. All three of my brothers were/are custodians. They are all single, and live together and never got more than a few miles from home. Their lives revolved around care- giving and serving others. And, I would like to add, they have been perfectly content and quite successful in doing just that. Plus, you could never find three finer, more giving, kind men than those three brothers of mine!

But, I often wonder why did I get the athletic talent and mental capacity to successfully develop athletic success in many young men's lives? It's taken many years and a personal relationship with Jesus Christ to find out that answer. So, here it is, my life's journey directly, from me to you.

EARLY YEARS

I grew up in a small town in southern Illinois, just 20 miles east of St. Louis, named Shiloh. It was more of a village, and our address was simply rural route number one. Deprived of even a post office and lying smack dab in the middle of two larger towns, O'Fallon and Belleville, our address was simply Rural Route 1, O'Fallon, IL.

At one point in time, Shiloh harbored barely 450 inhabitants. I feel even the average Wal-Mart has more employees than the total number of my townspeople back in the day. Everybody knew everybody else, and we were this little tight-knit community living together in the same vicinity.

We owned a little two-bedroom house with a basement, a beat-up old car, and had a Catholic upbringing. It was not much, but that was all we had.

My dad, who had a high school education, was a civil servant that was responsible for parts supply at Scott Air Force Base, which was based a mile from my home in Shiloh. My mom, with a 10th-grade education, was a homemaker. I had three brothers. Twins, Tim and Tom, who were three years younger than me, and the youngest brother, Jodie, was six years younger than me.

I remember when I was around six months old, my mother dropped an open baby pin into my mouth and I swallowed it! In those days, babies wore washable cloth diapers held together by tiny, gold safety pins. As she was changing my diaper, she was holding a baby pin in her mouth and it accidentally fell out of her mouth and into mine and I swallowed it. It was open!

Chaos! Panic ensued as you can imagine, and I was rushed to the emergency room. Daily X-rays were taken showing the pin moving around in my stomach.

A three-day timetable was given to pass it in my stool or surgery would be required. Wouldn't you know that on the third day it was found in my diaper stool? That gold safety pin was still open and it never got stuck. Incredible! It's times like these that when looking back, I can definitely see God's hand in my life.

Although I was raised Catholic and was an altar boy at church, I never had a personal relationship with Jesus. Not that I ever denied his existence, I just never knew the Lord. Yes, I went to confessions, but my relationship was more ritualistic based on going to church every Sunday. It was sitting, standing, and kneeling, rather than experiencing anything spiritual or personal at all.

Growing up, I would be embarrassed of my family's simple living conditions. We were six people living in a small, two-bedroom house. We had a kitchen with running water but no sink. Going over to my friends' and neighbors' houses and coming across a properly fitted kitchen would make me feel a sense of deprivation that I couldn't quite put into words.

Now, thinking back about this, I suppose you could say that I was definitely embarrassed.

I remember being twelve years old and crying myself to sleep about not being able to wait to get away from my home. You see, I never really experienced love and my home life experience was not a happy one.

I went to a catholic school on the grounds of St. John's Orphanage, which was right between Shiloh and Belleville. I learned under the supervision of nuns, who lived on the grounds of the orphanage. I didn't have many friends at school. Most of my friends were my cousins, neighbors, and non-catholic kids, who went to the public school. Growing up in a town as small as Shiloh, there weren't many kids the same age as me, so my friend circle was composed of kids of various ages. Our pastime involved us playing ball games in the summer. We played football, baseball, basketball, or just whatever sport happened to be in season.

I was always around baseball. I would go with my dad, who was umpiring little league games and play baseball with all the younger kids.

One particular memory that sticks out in my mind is when I was younger than six years of age and all the kids would congregate in the open field near the church to play baseball and they never let me play because I was too little. Based on my mom's memory, I would often kick up a big fuss. The crying had given way to a stubborn determination that had set in from that day forth. I was determined to play baseball, and I was going to succeed at it.

In 1960, I officially joined the Khoury league as a six-year-old. It was an organized baseball league named after a prominent man from our community, George Khoury. It had different age levels known as, Atoms, Bantams, Midgets, and Juveniles. Each level would consist of training for two years before proceeding to the next level. Atoms were the youngest teams and Juveniles were the oldest teams in the league.

The Atoms League had balls known as atom balls, which were smaller balls than the regular-sized baseballs to fit the kid's hands better. Now, I often talk about the science behind this ball size as a coach, when I train kids of the same age.

The Khoury League had three areas for their fields and followed a strict schedule for games. I remember getting my first real baseball uniform as a six-year-old and honestly thinking that this was like ten Christmases all wrapped up in one. Wow, I, Dave Jorn had an amazing and awesome baseball uniform! Simply, unbelievable! Actually, I probably would have worn that baseball uniform every day and would have slept in it at night, but I didn't want to stain or ruin it. I would imagine most of the guys reading this right now felt the same way about their first uniform.

But, sadly, I also remember being really embarrassed by my dad during my Khoury League days. When I was around ten years old, some of the parents would gather at a tavern after ball games, and the kids would play outside until dark and then come in to eat. A number of times when I would come in, I would see my dad standing on his head on top of the bar and could hear everyone laughing at him. My dad always seemed to be the life of any party when he had a couple of beers in him. That always bothered me and to this day my dad's actions continue to be quite vivid in my mind.

My fondest memories from this time are just getting atop my bicycle, riding down to the Shiloh ballpark with my glove and bat to play baseball, only to return home hours and hours later.

This was contrary to what my mom wanted. She would step out of our backdoor and yell "David" multiple times at the top of her lungs for me to come home. You see, she wanted to control what I did. But I, with my spirit of independence, which has served me well throughout my whole life, just ignored her call. I came home when I was ready to come home and not a minute earlier!

During my early years of playing baseball, I was always an infielder, only moving on to catching and shortstop in high school, before proceeding to pitch in junior college.

RELIGION AND FAMILY:

My paternal grandmother, who lived next door to us while growing up, used to bake coffee cakes for the priests and look after them. She had five children including my dad. My dad had a brother in St. Louis, two sisters in Belleville, Illinois, a brother in Salt Lake City, Utah, and another brother in California.

When my grandmother was alive, periodically, the entire family, including my parents and brothers, aunts, uncles, and cousins, congregated at my grandmother's house. It involved having amazingly competitive pinochle card games and was lots of fun! When she passed, everything just kind of fell apart. I feel she was saved for all her graciousness towards the men of God in the Catholic Church, but I don't know actually if she was born again or not.

Dad has since passed away, and my mom is now 90 years old and living in a nursing home and with all her nerve issues, she isn't doing too well, but I truly feel she is saved and will be in heaven for eternity.

My twin brothers are saved and constantly serving and doing things for others. My youngest brother, Jodie, I do have doubts about him and his salvation. Sadly he doesn't attend church on Sundays. And even though my wife, Melinda, witnessed to him a couple of years ago, and said he accepted Christ, I felt it was just for show, so he could get rid of her and move on. I know it sometimes takes a while before the message sinks in and changes your heart but I have never seen a change in Jodie. Like I mentioned earlier, we all did go to Saturday confession but never did it touch me at a deep level when I was younger and lived at home.

When my dad wasn't working, he would be gone a lot, and most often he would go to the bar. This lead to a lot of loneliness for my mom, and it impacted her in a deep way in which she formed an unhealthy attachment to my twin brothers. She wanted them to continually be with her and have no independence of their own. Mom never learned to drive and dad was gone a lot.

My mom tried smothering me when I was young, but my rebellious attitude would not let that happen. If she said, "NO" or "you can't", I did it anyway. That's not something I recommend, but in my case it allowed me to have independence and flourish.

One example of my "independence" or "rebellious attitude" was whenever my mom would tell me NOT to go to the woods for fear of catching poison ivy which I was allergic to, and all my friends were going to the woods, I would follow my friends and not pay attention to her nagging or the possibility of catching poison ivy. I would just go!

HIGH SCHOOL

After eighth grade, I went to a Catholic High School in Belleville. I was just one of two kids from Shiloh that attended there.

In my freshman year, I was barely 5 feet tall and weighed only 90 pounds. I tried out for basketball and made the freshman team, but never played. Then I tried out for freshman baseball and got cut. In my sophomore year, I tried out for basketball and baseball. Even though I was 5 feet and 2 inches tall and weighed 92 pounds, I thought I was really big! Haha, I never thought I would grow. I tried out for baseball and got cut again and that's when I decided that I was never going back there again. I could simply not put up with being rejected time and time again when I knew in my heart I was good enough to be playing.

In the two long years that I wasn't playing for my high school, I still had my Khoury League, and I eventually made it as far as the Juvenile League.

My love for baseball was not at all limited to being selected for and making the school team. I knew my time would eventually come. The key was just to keep trying and waiting. And yes, the waiting was quite painful, especially for a teenager who lacked patience.

I decided to move to O'Fallon High School as most of my friends attended there. At the start of my junior year, my first physical was due. Amazingly, I had grown a total of 9 inches over the year, from 5' 2" to 5' 11". That's where things took a turn for the best for me, From not being recognized at all in my previous years due to being tiny, I was suddenly the starting shortstop on the baseball team! Also, I became the starting point guard on the junior varsity basketball team. Man, was I excited! And, deep down in my heart, I knew I deserved this because of all the time and hard work I had put into both of these sports.

One time, I was voted as high school player of the week and this was announced in the local newspaper. That was a time I felt, wow, I have finally hit the jackpot! And, I realized later that the Lord had blessed me with much physical ability and talent. Also, I was realizing my deep determination and resilience were paying off in many ways.

My dad was supportive of my love for sports. Way before I had ever proved anything, he bought me a really nice Rawlings baseball glove. The glove was expensive and I know my dad was using money we really didn't have to buy it.

All three of my younger brothers displayed no interest whatsoever in sports. Although the twins made an effort to specifically attend the events that involved me, it was clear they never really enjoyed participating in any of the games. All three eventually shared the same fate, they received a high school education, all became custodians, they never married and to this day, they all live together in the same house. But, I do feel they are happy helping one another.

There are times when I have wondered why I was spared the same lifestyle as my three brothers, Why did I end up in better circumstances? Better circumstances I had determined in my own mind. At least in my own way of thinking, because they were and continue to be quite happy and content in their own lives. I kept wondering where I fit in this family. Many times, I thought, perhaps I am adopted, but that's not at all possible because I look just like my mom. Most often it seemed like, in this household, God had pointed his finger at me and chose me to do great things. As I said, I had never had a personal relationship with God and I often wondered, why has he been so kind to me? At this point and time in my life, God had orchestrated my life from day one and I just had not realized it yet!

COLLEGE

As the times and seasons of life went by, the time had finally arrived for me to graduate high school. As the day approached, I knew that my next step would be going to college. And the one place I had set my sights set on was Southern Illinois University, SIU-Carbondale. Back in the day, that was the place for baseball. I was 6'1, 145 pounds, and playing shortstop, but I did not have any offers whatsoever to go there. Feeling a bit dejected, I chose to stay close to home, and attend Belleville Junior College, now Southwestern Illinois College -SWIC.

For me, junior college was far more fun than serious. It was all about partying and playing baseball. Class attendance was quite rare for me. I knew what I needed to do in the classroom to be eligible to transfer and I did only the bare minimum to accomplish that.

And in 1972, that same year, my grandfather (mom's stepfather) bought me a 64' Chevy Malibu which was my first car. Boy, I thought I had it going on now! Driving a hot car and an athlete starting on the varsity baseball team.

I wasn't very keen on playing basketball in college and concentrated and put all my effort into baseball. I was 6'1 and 145 pounds when I started college in the fall, but by the spring I had put on 30lbs and now weighed 175lbs. I was definitely a late bloomer. Actually, I should have still been a senior in high school when I entered college. I did not turn 18 until October of my freshman year in college.

I played shortstop in my freshman year in junior college, Then, the summer of 1973 taught me that I really wasn't much of a hitter at all. I played in a summer collegiate league called the CICL (Central Illinois Collegiate League) in Macomb, IL. And I only hit around 200 that summer. I could really throw, so I was asked to pitch one day that summer towards the end of the season, as we were short on pitchers. I think I might have pitched a total of two or three innings.

In the spring of 1974, I had broken my thumb playing basketball and I couldn't hit any longer, Now, I could only pitch. That's the spring when I pitched probably 20 innings and received a $500 scholarship to go to Southeast Missouri State (SEMO).

After two years of junior college, I proceeded to Southeast Missouri State as an incoming junior. I lived on campus with a teammate of mine from junior college. I worked at the Greek cafeteria and got free meals since I worked there. This was a huge deal, it helped me save a lot on expenses because I really had no money at all. Again, even though I didn't realize it, the Lord was providing for me and for my future.

My first year at SEMO did not go well. I never saw the mound and decided I would transfer to a NAIA college near my home, so I could play in the field and also pitch. I loved playing and that year at SEMO was all but satisfying. I was used to playing and having to sit on the bench was doing everything but killing me. The more I thought about transferring, the more I knew I couldn't quit. I never quit anything. I definitely was not a quitter! So, back I went, determined in my final year that I would be the best that I could be.

Fall ball 1975 started and we had some quality returning players and some talented new recruits, which truly meant I had to work harder than ever before. Intrasquad games began and this was my chance to step up and prove my worth. When the lineups were posted, the coach always had me pitching against the starting lineup and the pitchers who pitched all the innings the previous year pitching against the "B" team. The more I thought about how I had the deck stacked against me, the madder I got.

I remember being extremely angry every time I would go to view the roster and the line-up for the day. I was always the one pitching against the starting lineup. This would get me agitated and wound up. I would go to the baseball field really angry and try to intimidate the other team. I took the mound in anger and if anyone mouthed off from the dugout I would drill them or at least knock them down. Remember that I had a really good arm and threw hard. Nobody wanted to hit off me because I would mow them down.

I won lots of pitching time the next spring due to my showing in the Fall. Unfortunately, my results were not nearly as good as in the Fall. It took my teammate, Mark Hogan, to help me figure out that I lacked the fire and anger I had in the Fall, and once I figured out how to get that back, I flourished. I had to pitch angrily and with an attitude. We rolled through the MIAA (Missouri Intercollegiate Conference). Our team was loaded. And I was proud to be able to say that I was one of the main reasons our team had been so successful. Little did I know, the Lord was polishing me for a career in baseball, the absolute love of my life!

After the season was over, we won the league championship but due to the lack of automatic bids in the postseason play, we had to go home. It wasn't possible to stay on campus and practice since the program lacked the funds to keep us there. Three days later, we hear that we have received a bid to a regional in St. Louis. We celebrated by going back into town to the Sprig Street Tavern. It was a celebration involving playing pool, drinking beer, and doing shots. Man, I felt my life was really going well.

Nearly the entire team was there, we were all pumped up, but not one of my wisest decisions as it turned out. I got pulled over for driving under the influence of alcohol and had to have my coach bail me out. If my poor choice wasn't bad enough, it put Coach Uhls in a tough spot regarding one of his best pitchers. I think coach knew though that most of his team was out that night and almost all of them had participated in the partying at the bar. Rather than make the decision on what to do about me, he put it up to the team to decide. What a move! I have been forever grateful to him for that. Now, I had even more reason to be the best. Well, we breezed through the regional and went on to the DII World Series. I won a game in the regional and pitched game one of the World Series. I gave up three runs in the top of the first inning and put our team in a tough spot. We battled back and won 4-3 in ten innings. I would definitely not be denied and pitched all ten innings for the win. This win was one of the most satisfying wins in my whole baseball career.

PLAYING

I wasn't ever bothered by school since I was always obsessed with baseball. I wouldn't ever apply myself in school and would just get grades that would get me by and that was all. My parents and family never pressured me about my grades or anything and I definitely wasn't in the race to be a doctor or engineer. I was only concerned with playing baseball. After we came in third at the Division II World Series, I got an invite to go to a tryout camp at Busch Stadium for the Cardinals. I grew up a Cardinal's fan and this stadium was only twenty minutes from my home. I was extremely excited to pitch on Bob Gibson's mound. They let each of us pitch two innings. I went out there and struck out five guys and got a pop-up on the infield and the scout who was running this camp, Fred McAllister, approached me and said that it looks like I have a good arm, but they cannot tell how hard I was throwing without a radar gun. Back in those days and times, radar guns weren't a dime a dozen as they are today!

Fred McAllister told me they were holding a tryout camp the next weekend in Little Rock, Arkansas, at Ray Winder Field, the Cardinals AA (Double-A) affiliate. I had nothing to lose and everything to gain, as I was out of college eligibility and desperately wanted to play pro ball. The scout, Mr. McAllister told me if I threw 85 on the radar gun he would sign me. So I drove down to Little Rock, which was a seven-hour drive. The Cardinals paid for my gas and meals and put me up in a hotel when I got to Little Rock. The next day I went down to the ballpark where Fred asked me when I was ready to throw. I told him I needed to loosen up a bit first and I would prefer to go third or fourth so he let me take my time. As it turned out, I pitched a couple of innings and the radar showed 87 to 89, which in today's radars, which register higher, would have shown 91 to 93mph. The thing was, I wasn't even throwing as hard as I did back at Busch Stadium, so he signed me and gave me a $500 bonus. I drove back home excited and ended up getting a speeding ticket in Paragould, Arkansas, and $75 out of my signing bonus was now gone. They sent me to Sarasota, Florida, as part of the Gulf Coast League, which is a Cardinals Rookie Ball League. The year was 1976.

FIRST IMPRESSIONS:

The year was 1976. There were 17 pitchers on the pitching staff and just a lot of guys everywhere, so the atmosphere was extremely competitive. I had two signature pitches, a four-seam fastball, and a dirty curveball. No one had ever taught me pitching mechanics or pitches and it was just what had been developed in me over the years. The coaches wanted me to learn to throw a two-seam fastball and learn how to throw a slider. This meant unlearning everything I had innately built up within me over the years. I know it was easy for them to let me go if I didn't adjust because I was just a $500 investment to them, nothing big. Nobody questioned orders back in those days and if they told you to do something, you just did what they asked you to do and trusted they knew what was best for you. So, I did what they asked me to do, I struggled, but I persisted because I had a hard-bent determination in me and I worked hard to develop those pitches. Day in and day out, while playing catch,

I started to get the feel for the two new pitches they had asked me to develop.

THE YEAR AFTER:

The next year, I was sent to Class A, in Gastonia, North Carolina. It was a low-Class A League called the Western Carolina League (now known as the South Atlantic League). I had a really good year and finished the season with an 8 and 1 record. But, due to tendinitis in my elbow, I was out for six weeks.

After the season, I was invited to the Instructional League. I was thrilled because back in the 70s, the Instructional League was strictly reserved for players they thought were the twenty-five best prospects in their organization. This wasn't for Double-A or Triple-A guys. It was mostly for Class A and Rookie Ball guys who were brought there for future development. The Instructional League had a lot of instructors to help facilitate your progress and just like nowadays, they had a hitting coach, a pitching coach, and a defensive coach. However, in those days, for each ball club, there was only one coach who was also your manager. Roving coaches would come into each of the team's farm clubs for five days at a time to teach as well as to evaluate. Then, they would come back to town, later on, to see what skills you had improved on. Therefore, Instructional League was an upgrade with so many coaches for different needs and all the players got to work on honing their key skills and specializations. It was definitely an excellent situation for me to be in and I took full advantage of the situation.

The Instructional League lasted two months (nowadays it isn't more than four weeks) and I did great there. I was given amazing feedback and it was made known to me that I could make it to Double-A. At that moment, I was in the low A-League in Gastonia, and high A was in St. Petersburg, Florida, and in the Florida State League. Double-A for me meant returning to Little Rock, where I was signed, and the prospect of that extremely excited me.

CHALLENGES

I went to spring training and pitched for Double A Little Rock. Spring training in those days was in St. Petersburg, Florida. During the last week, I got caught in the shuffle. There were around forty guys in the major league camp and they only take twenty-five, which meant fifteen had to be let go or sent down to AAA. It's very competitive and a lot of guys were older and more experienced than me, too. The way events unfolded was that the Triple-A guys got demoted to Double-A and I got bumped down to St. Petersburg which was kind of okay because it was a high Class A league. 1978, I started the season 7-0, but tendinitis showed up in my elbow again and I was out for four weeks and ended up finishing the season 10-3. I had gone from Rookie Ball to High-Class A. So naturally, I was expecting to make it to Double-A. So, in 1979 I went to spring training for Double-A Ball, but at the end of spring training, I get bumped back down to St. Petersburg. I was genuinely not happy about this at all. I had been given no reason as to why I was back in A ball. I was twenty-four years old and the clock was ticking and ticking fast. The management didn't have much of an investment in me. I was disposable to them, and hence it was extremely easy to overlook me.

In my mind, I had nothing to prove in A ball. I was 18-4 in two years of class A ball and had proved that level was easy. I learned how to manage my elbow, going a full season without any inflammation, because I had learned how to prevent any future problems. All I needed to do was stretch my elbow out, so I did that with a ten-pound dumbbell on a daily basis and never faced any elbow issues ever again. I finished 10-9 that year and knowing myself, I could have won twenty games easily had I really put my heart and mind into it, but I had a poor old me attitude and was feeling sorry for myself. This was not where I was meant to be. To me, staying in A class was wasting time. I needed to prove myself at the next level.

Around three quarters into the season, the farm director comes to watch us play and he is the guy responsible for deciding who goes where and does what. I decided that I needed to show him that I didn't belong there, I belonged in double-A, and I pitched like I was capable and had a great game.

After everyone went home, I waited in the locker room to be called into the manager's office because that's where the manager and farm director were engaged in talks. I figured they would call me in and discuss moving me up to Double-A. I waited in the locker room for over an hour without any call, so I stood up, knocked on the office door, and asked if I could come in and speak with them. I was let inside and the farm director mentioned how well I pitched that day, I told him that's what I came to discuss with him in detail. I asked him what more the team expected of me to move to Double-A since I had already proved myself worthy in A ball by winning so many games. The response was blunt, "We don't have any room for you in Double-A". I calmly suggested that perhaps somewhere there would be room in Double-A and they could use me, a good pitcher in their league.

The farm director stood right over me, brought his face real close to mine, and blurted out, "You don't want to be a Cardinal."

I lost it! I stood up and spoke loud and clear that I am more a Cardinal than he ever could be because I grew up literally 20 minutes from St. Louis and all my life all I ever wanted to do was pitch for the Cardinals. This exchange was incredibly heated because I was all fired up and the manager had to break us apart. I left the office thinking I was done for, and I would soon be released. My career as a baseball player would be over for good.

After the season finished, a surprise awaited me, I didn't get released! Instead, I went to spring training with Double-A in Little Rock, Arkansas. I pitched well in the Spring Training and made the Double-A team. Finally! This was 1980 and I was officially starting my career in Double-A Little Rock, where it all started for me.

Later on, I discovered that I had gone to Little Rock Double-A on the disabled list even though I was not injured! A friend of mine, Dave England, who is now a retired trainer for the Razorbacks, told me that the manager stood up for me and wouldn't let the farm director release me. He liked me and respected me. He saved my career because he saw, in me, a passion to excel. His name was Sonny Roberto.

So perhaps, standing up for myself in that office was the right thing to do after all. And the fire in my eyes and passion in my soul to see myself in a greater spotlight, brought me closer to my dreams. Now here I had finally made it to Double-A to the place my professional career had actually started at Ray Winder Field.

During those days, we would play an exhibition game against the Razorbacks prior to the start of the season. I was running in the outfield a day before we were to play the Razorbacks and ended up pulling my groin muscle. I knew that I was dispensable since I am on the disabled list, and not injured, and if I was to tell the trainer I had any problem, I would never get off the disabled list. I sucked it up, dealt with the pain, shortened my stride just a bit to not bother my pulled groin, and pitched against the Razorbacks. I ended up pitching six shutout innings against the team that has just been to the College World Series for the first time in 1979. A short time later, I finally came off the disabled list. To me, that was another lesson in using every chance I could get to prove myself, pain or no pain.

In 1980, we played the Dodgers and won the Texas League Championship in San Antonio, Texas. I was not on the roster for the championship because I had torn a ligament in my knee while pinch-running for our catcher earlier in the year. Being a pretty good athlete and former position player, I had done this a couple of times and actually also pinch-hit a couple of times. So, I needed to get more innings pitched after the season ended and I was sent to winter ball in Mazatlan, Mexico. There, I was used as a starter and reliever between starts. My arm didn't react well to this, and I got tendinitis in my shoulder, so here we go again, another injury sidetracks me and I head home to rehab and get ready for spring training in 1981.

I came back but never went to see a doctor. I just expected it to pass like my normal injuries. I mean, being an athlete means having to deal with injuries at all points in your career. This is why most players don't ever make it to the big leagues. Apart from the basic lack of talent and desire, the many injuries don't let you play beyond a certain point. For me, I had accumulated a series of injuries. First, it was the tendinitis in my elbow. Second, it was a pulled knee ligament. Third, it was my groin and now it was my shoulder. I was gradually becoming noticeably injured. Could I stay healthy long enough to be able to play? That was the book on me and I knew what the Cardinals were thinking.

So, after returning from Mexico, I tried my best to rehab my shoulder in time for spring training and I felt I was doing okay. In spring training of 1981, I was sent back to Double A. Everything was okay and I got off to a great start. I think I had something like twenty-four consecutive scoreless innings pitched to start the season. So they sent me to Triple-A and I felt my shoulder aching again like it did when I was in Mexico. While throwing around eighty miles an hour and getting hit around pretty well, I started treating myself. I couldn't afford to let anyone know I was hurting but I guess it was pretty obvious. At any rate, I had my own ice pack, and heating pad and was taking anti-inflammatory drugs. The best game I pitched was the second game of a doubleheader. My buddy, Danny Winslow, was the catcher and he knew me well.

Danny Winslow and I had signed the same year, in 1976. He had come straight out of high school and I was a few years older, but he was really mature and we lived together quite a few times whenever we were on the same team. That day in 1981, we won the game. I had given up one hit. At that time, I was on aspirin and DMSO (an FDA-approved prescription drug to deal with pain) to deal with my inflammation. Again, I had my own ice pack, my own heating pad, and a DMSO pack. I kept all of these things without telling anyone, even the trainer. I didn't want anybody to find out about my injury, but that day, my below-average performance gave me away. I was capable of so much more and just wasn't just able to perform, the velocity just wasn't there. Not long after that, I got sent back down to Double-A.

My time in Double-A was full of injury issues. I used to be a starter, but now I wasn't. Most often I would be found in the bullpen. I was in the position known as long reliever and this was not entirely ideal. Every day I would wake up with my shoulder killing me. As a long reliever, you get up in the bullpen early in the game when the starter struggles. I had a few of these up and downs without getting into the game and it really bothered my shoulder. I finally got to start and pitched 6 innings. Then, I woke up with a frozen shoulder the next day. It was throbbing with pain and I could not move my arm at all. Definitely, not a situation I had planned on being in!

My shoulder had frozen so badly that I was unable to move my arm alongside it. I ended up at the doctor where he gave me a cortisone shot. This helped to lubricate my shoulder joints. The bursa sac in my shoulder had totally filled with fluid. I finished the season and knew my days were numbered. You only last for a short time in the minor leagues when you are injury-prone. And, I had become just that, prone to injuries. In my cognizant mind, I knew my dream of playing and pitching in the major leagues was all but over.

During the off-season, instead of attempting to play with my multitude of injuries, I decided to finish my degree. I needed only one class, physiology, to get my degree and I took the class and graduated that year in 1981.

I had started my degree in 1972 and it had taken me almost a decade to graduate. I always knew I could go back and finish my degree when baseball was over, and it did end in October 1981. Got my pink slip (release paper), very impersonal, no call just a letter. I eventually felt everything happened the way it did so that things could fall into place at their appointed time. And, as I look back at things, I know the Lord was lining things up for me.

Minor league baseball is not as glamorous as you might think. The ballparks, travel, and money, are a lot better now than in my days, which was not much and you would only get paid during the playing season, which runs from April (post-spring training) to September (season's end).

In the off-season, you had to find a part-time job while trying to work out and be ready for the next year's season. I had a lot of fun in the off-season in 1981. Brad Harriman, my friend was an assistant basketball coach at a high school and he asked if I would be interested in coaching the sophomore team. I definitely knew some basketball, so I told him "Yes". That year, my team finished the season 16-6, won our sophomore tournament, and had a blast doing it. I played all my players. Winning is and always will be important, but not at the expense of the kids' confidence, not at that age. That was something that I had learned the hard way when I was a kid myself. And, within my power, it wouldn't happen to another young athlete the way it had happened to me.

THE TRANSITION YEAR WITH MY FRIEND, MARK HOGAN

Mark Hogan and I had become best friends over time. Despite going through college together, we never got real close during our college days. One morning in 1978, in St. Petersburg, Florida, I ended up running into him while having lunch at Luby's cafeteria. Right across the table from mine, there sat my old teammate, Mark. There he was with me in St. Petersburg!

I asked him what he was doing there. He was painting apartments for a living, which wasn't exactly a cushy job. He desperately wanted to re-enter the world of baseball but didn't know exactly how to do this. It was during those days that he would attend my games and we would almost always hang out after every single game. That brought us to be close friends.

Fall of 1979, Mark went to Mississippi State to work under legendary college coach, Ron Polk, and graduated with a master's degree. After his internship as a graduate assistant, he got a high school job in the panhandle of Florida. So on my way to spring training the next couple of years, 1980 & 1981, I would stop off in Crestview, Florida, and stay with Mark and Becky (his wife) and their first daughter, Julie Jean. This gave me a chance to visit with my friend and to get outside to work out and get ready for spring training. The weather in Jan./Feb. is not very conducive to working out in Illinois.

After I got released back in 1981, Mark Hogan got a job as head coach in the spring of 1982 at Lurleen B. Wallace Community College. He invited me to come down and help him with his pitchers, which was my first opportunity to coach. I lived with Mark, Becky, and Julie. I would coach pitchers in the afternoon and a college booster gave me an hourly job doing odd jobs in the morning. Thanks to living with the Hogan family, I was able to barely keep my head above water and survive.

I really enjoyed coaching. I had learned so much about baseball and pitching that I was eager to share it with young players. The Cardinals taught me the game of baseball. Specifically, Hub Kittle taught me pitching and George Kissel for the positional player part. Just before the season ended, Mark suggested that I put together a resume and send it to several college baseball coaches. It had been the road he had traveled when he got a graduate position at Mississippi State. Baseball had always been a part of my life, so it was a no-brainer to try to continue as a coach.

From the resumes that I had sent out, I had responses from a few coaches, but the one that stood out for me was the one from the University of Arkansas. I had spent parts of two summers in Little Rock and liked the state. Plus, it was where I started my professional career after the try-out camp in Little Rock. Coach Norm DeBriyn, the head baseball coach at the University of Arkansas, offered me a job as their pitching coach. I jumped at the opportunity and in the summer of 1982, I officially became a Razorback. Although I had all the responsibilities of a full-time coach, I was paid as a graduate assistant. Doug Clark was the only full-time paid assistant, so I was paid $400 a month and my master's classes were paid for, also.

Being only 28 years old and single at the time, I was able to make do but not without the help of Coach DeBriyn and Coach

Clark. After rent, utilities, car insurance, and other expenses, the $400 didn't last long. I was invited often to the coach's houses to eat dinner and they practically made me a part of their families. I look back now and realize just how blessed I truly was.

COACHING

When I started out as an assistant coach in 1982 at the University of Arkansas, I was barely twenty-eight years old. Because of my youth and inexperience, my approach to coaching was tough love. My past experiences had toughened me up a lot. I mean, I had been denied all the way through my experience in baseball. I was denied freshman basketball and baseball and then sophomore basketball and baseball. I had to try out multiple times to eventually get signed by a Rookie ball league with a bare minimum sign-on bonus of $500. And, at the U of A, I wanted the student-athletes to value their scholarships and work hard to prove themselves.

I was tough on the kids. First, as I said, I didn't want to be taken advantage of because I was just a few years their senior. And secondly, because their personal best had been set way too low for them in the past. Plus, they had no idea what a world of sharks awaited them if they were ever to enter the professional arena. Always in the back of my mind, I dreamed of making it to the College World Series. I wanted to make my mark as a coach and show the world that I was capable of accomplishing my goals. My team's success directly pointed to my success as a college pitching coach.

Eventually, as time progressed, and as I matured in the coaching profession, it became less about me and more about the players and their futures. Yet again, the dilemma was, what could my team accomplish with my influence? So I didn't let them rest. One time, in 1982, during my first Fall season, I felt things weren't going in the right direction and that the culture needed to change from happy to be here, to pay the price of succeeding and winning. So, I forced the team to run until it was after dark and they had to run 75 foul poles. It didn't take that long for the leaders on the team to step up and stop the others from complaining and for them to do their part for the whole team to be successful.

Looking back on my student years, I was more of a sponge for information. I would listen to pitching coaches, field coaches, base running coaches, hitting coaches, and literally anyone with the experience and maturity who had some baseball knowledge to offer me. I wanted to know how to do rundowns and defensive stuff and everything about the baseball game I loved. Any athlete with coaching in their future agenda, should always be a sponge and learn everything they possibly can!

I was definitely tough on my players as a coach. I had been trained in the Cardinal Organization with the best coaches, and I expected and desired for my team to benefit from my past training and experiences.

The Cardinal's organization had a great baseball man working for them, known as George Kissel. He was phenomenal for teaching all aspects of the game of baseball. It was due to his efforts that I ended up having great pitching coaches such as Hub Kittel and Bo Miliken. Also, I had other teaching coaches there who knew how to keep things simple and continually tried to adapt these things to their players. I intended to instill these same principles into my players too.

My constant and never-ending hunger for the knowledge of the game of baseball in my earlier years meant that as an assistant coach, I knew a lot about the fundamentals and the game, and I could teach and implement all of these things to my players as well. My experience and baseball personality took over as a coach and I wanted these kids to understand there was a price you have to pay to be good. And if they wanted to be "good", they had to be willing to pay that price, no matter the cost!

I truly understood from the beginning of my career that baseball was more of a mental game than just a physical game. You could be the best player in terms of physical tools, however, it took mental strength and stability to win. I ensured my pitchers that they would develop both mental toughness and competitiveness through my coaching and training.

1983 was the only year that we, the University of Arkansas Razorback's Baseball team, didn't make a post-season bid. After 1983, the next time we didn't make a bid wasn't until the year 2016. Yes, you heard me correctly, from the year 1984 to 2015, we successfully made a post-season bid for the NCAA Baseball Championship. But I was in pro baseball from 1989-2002, more on that later. My only post-season bid misses were my first and last year as a coach at the University of Arkansas. Of course, this covered my two stints at Arkansas. These were a result of our efforts on the field. We fought tooth and nail for these results. The long hours all paid off and I couldn't be more proud of all we achieved as a result of this hard work. There were lots of great kids I trained and great people I worked alongside. Of course, all the success we achieved would not have been possible without the confidence and trust that Coach Debriyn and Coach Van Horn had and put in me. All of our success is a reflection of the commitment of the coaches and players to the sport of college baseball. I consider it an honor and a privilege the Lord has blessed me with such a successful coaching career that I had with the Arkansas Razorbacks. And, that I've been able to coach with such creative and winning coaches as Norm Debriyn, and Dave Van Horn, and have rubbed shoulders with, and become friends with some of the greatest coaches in the SEC, SWC, and the whole baseball college nation. Many thanks to my Lord for all that He has blessed me with, and continues to bless me to this day!

During the winter of 1985 and the off-season at the University of Arkansas baseball, I went to El-Salvador with the United States Information Agency to coach, and give clinics and lessons to the kids in El-Salvador. I had no idea about the political uncertainty and turmoil there. It was the year when the marines were gunned down in Zona Rosa, El-Salvador. I got picked up at the airport by the cultural attaché in a station wagon. I tried looking out the windows and realized it was bulletproof glass all around me and I couldn't see a thing. Thankfully, I was placed in a nice hotel and it was such a scenic tropical climate there. Everywhere I turned my head, I could see the natural beauty created by God.

My first day there was actually scary. I had showered, and dressed, and I had taken an elevator from the fourth floor to the reception area. The only other person in the elevator with me was Salvadoran. Riding on the elevator, somewhere between the second and third floor, we heard gunfire and the elevator stopped, and it went all black inside. I was totally freaking out and the native guy did the weirdest thing, he started whistling at the top of his lungs. I could not help but feel terrified as to what was going on. Whose attention was this guy trying to get? He didn't speak English and I didn't know enough Spanish to communicate. Was I going to make it out of there alive? We were stuck inside for thirty minutes before finally being rescued. Later, I found out that the Salvadoran rebels had bombed electricity grid stations just to cause inconvenience to the innocent people living in their country. Now, looking back on this incident, I know the Lord protected me another time in my life and to look to Him for safety and protection.

I couldn't help but wonder what I had gotten myself into that day. I had gone to El Salvador with no security, and all on my own. Thankfully, there were a few local kids who had traveled here to attend English colleges and could help translate things for me while I was there and when I needed help.

I was taken to their baseball fields, to what they simply called "fields". Running on the fields was like running on a sandy beach. On the "fields", they didn't have anything even closely resembling a pitching mound.

I was there for only two weeks. So, I took a bunch of baseballs, some old gloves, and some catcher's gear with me and passed them out at the mini camps we were holding. The kids absolutely loved it! These were underprivileged kids with an immense love for the game of baseball. They would play with electrical tape wrapped around the well-used balls. These taped-up balls would have been trashed in the good ole USA. But here they were just thrilled to have a few used-up baseballs to play with.

I did camps for the kids and showed them how to field ground balls and how to hit off tees. It was amazing working with them. They were so happy and full of life. They were thankful for every simple thing in their lives. We all should be more thankful for our lives filled with blessings, as these underprivileged kids were.

I even attended a Halloween party while I was there. I was in San Salvador, the capital, and I went to a marine base to attend the party. I remember before our car drove up at the base, they did a security sweep underneath the car looking for bombs. For me, this concept was new, but it taught me how serious security was here and how I was wonderfully fortunate to live in the United States. The party was great and I even made several new friends! Quickly, the two weeks in El Salvador ended and I flew back to America.

Now, it was the winter of 1986 and as I mentioned earlier, I had always wondered if I could ever possibly be a major league pitching coach. In my mind, the path I had mapped out involved me working with and coaching minor league baseball teams and gradually working my way up as I gained experience and knowledge. And, through this, I should be able to gain enough positive recognition to move up to major league baseball. All I had to do was close my eyes and see myself on the mound of a major league baseball team giving advice to a big-league pitcher.

In the summer of 1988, I got an opportunity to work in professional baseball. It was supposed to be a one-time thing where the NCAA allows coaches to figure out if professional ball is really for them. It wasn't against any NCAA rules or so we were told. Coach DeBriyn let me travel to Johnson City, Tennessee, which is in the Appalachian Minor League. It was a farm team for the St. Louis Cardinals, who I had played for in my six-year minor league career. A month or so later, I received an urgent call from Coach DeBriyn telling me that the NCAA was actually not okay with this arrangement and I had to leave. Despite the fact that I had to leave so soon, I was there long enough to know in my heart that this was the place for me. This is what I needed to do and wanted to do with my life. My true desire was to be a major league pitching coach!

I returned to the University of Arkansas and coached through the fall of 1988. During this time, I sent out my resume to several professional organizations hoping to get a job in professional baseball. I heard back from a couple of clubs, one of which was the New York Yankees. They made an offer, an offer I decided to accept.

I resigned as the University of Arkansas pitching coach and in January, 1989, I began working for the New York Yankees. My dreams were coming to fruition. I, David Alan Jorn, small-town boy from Illinois, was going to be coaching professional baseball! Yes, my dreams were coming true!

I was assigned to Prince William Virginia, a bedroom community of Washington DC, which was in the Carolina League, a Class A team. Spring training didn't start until March, so I headed back to the St. Louis area on the Illinois side and bought a condo there getting myself ready to go to spring training. Next, I moved on to spring training in Tampa, Florida, with the Yankees. We broke camp and went to Prince William. Guess what! We ended up winning the league championship in 1989. In my head, I was thinking, Dave, job well done!

One of my good friends, Trey Hillman, was the hitting instructor there at the time. Eventually, he and I went to South Korea together to coach in 2017. Now, I know and realize how Jesus was putting certain people in my life to actually make a plan for my life.

It was a really fun year for me because it was my first real taste of coaching professional baseball and we ended up champions, which is the best ending any baseball team and season could possibly have. But, the excitement quickly ended for me when I heard the terrible news that one of my best friends had committed suicide. I returned home for the funeral. A sad ending to a thrilling year for me. And, the Lord was making me have lots of questions and thoughts as to why someone would take their own life.

In 1990, I was sent to Greensboro, North Carolina, but we didn't win any league championships. And in the winter, I ended up in Venezuela. So thankful to find out that Valenzuela was a democracy and a very civilized and cultured nation that carried with them a great love for baseball. Safety and baseball in my life! What more could I ask for?

The crowds in Venezuela were electric. Three-piece bands would be playing live music in the concourse stands, you could always hear whistling and bantering in the stands, and the moment the game starts, instantly, everyone is glued to their seats watching the ballgame while drinking beer and enjoying the game.

There would be chicken wire all around the ballpark, from dugout to dugout, to help prevent the crowd from throwing things at you. As I said, the fans were passionate and very rowdy. They were liable to do all sorts of crazy things after drinking a few beers along with the excitement of the games.

In Venezuela, I was working with a team called Magallanes. We were coaching for the Yankees but the way it worked was that the Yankees and Magallanes had an agreement. The Yankees would send some of their players along with their coaches to Magallanes so that they could have five imports or foreigners on each team that was playing in the winter league.

The stadium bowl would have 25,000 loud fans and the Caracas mascot, which was a lion, would have his lion roar played over the PA system and the crowd would just go insanely wild. I would be standing directly next to my pitcher trying to settle him in and I had to yell as loud as I possibly could just for him to be able to hear me. It was truly deafening! But, really exciting for everyone at the baseball game, coaches, players, and spectators alike!

Sometimes, I felt there was a bit of a language barrier, but then I decided that there was no better way to communicate with your team than being right in the middle of everything. I didn't find Spanish that difficult to understand or speak and most of the team spoke basic English so we all got by pretty well on the bits and pieces of both English and Spanish that we all spoke and put together.

Spring training in 1991 took me to Albany, New York, and to the Eastern League, with the Yankees, Double-A league. I was moving up the ladder from A ball to Double-A ball and we even won the league championship that year in Harrisburg and had a very nice celebration in the locker room with all the coaches and players.

Sadly, that same year though, a player died. And that was an extremely painful time for me as a coach. His name was Jeff Hoffman and he was with me in Greensboro in 1990. He was very talented and a very competitive player. He had met a girl and got married in Greensboro in the offseason of 1990. Unknowingly, Jeff had cardiomyopathy and died quite suddenly.

On a road trip to Binghamton, a Mets team, I would bring the pitchers in early to get their work in. The hotel was within walking distance to the ballpark so they could head on over when they wanted to. It was the middle of summer, and extremely hot so we got our work in before the position players got there for batting practice (BP). That way, they, the pitchers, could shower, relax and cool down before the game started.

I was in the bullpen and Hoffy, Jeff Hoffman was supposed to work with me and I am looking around for him and he isn't anywhere to be seen. This was extremely unusual because Hoffy was an early bird and he would always be there on time, or early, no matter what. So I asked his roommate, Sterling Hitchcock, known as Hitchy. "Hitchy, where's Hoffy?" Hitchy told me that when he left, Hoffy was taking a shower and getting ready to come over to the ballpark. We decided to go on and wait for him to turn up. We thought perhaps he had gotten caught up in something personal. Our pre-workout went by, and we were in the middle of batting practice when suddenly the police showed up at the ballpark wanting to speak to the manager of our team.

The coaches collected in the locker room where the police broke the news to us, Hoffy was found dead in the hotel room by the maid.

The team was called in to update them about what had happened. The game was canceled while we all tried to process what had just occurred. The pitchers got together in my room to share our grief and Hitchy narrated a story that made us even more emotional.

We had come to Binghamton earlier in the season and played a series that Hoffy was part of. So, while staying in the exact same hotel room, Hoffy had received a call from his wife telling him he was going to be a father. And the next time we came to Binghamton to play, he passed away in the same hotel room where he found out that he was going to be a dad for the first time. We found out that he had undiagnosed cardiomyopathy. When he got out of the shower, he experienced a massive heart attack and just passed away on the bathroom floor.

The Yankees took the entire team to the funeral in Grand Rapids, Michigan. And in the same year, 1991, we went on to win the league championships, and we did it in memory of Jeff Hoffman.

My next coaching venture was winter ball in Venezuela again, and as usual, the games were all very competitive and consisted of a lot of major league players.

When I went back to Venezuela in the winter of 1991, I was affiliated with a different team in a different, smaller town, Maracay, Venezuela. The two major teams in Venezuela at that point in time were Magallanes and Caracas. It was a great place to be, with great foods, and drinkable water, but still with the same nutty, wild crowds. One time, we had an 11 a.m. game, and the fans all turned up wild and drunk.

Our team was getting hammered that day and the crowds were unhappy. So we brought in a Class A pitcher. This league had lots of Major League Baseball, AAA, and AA players in it and it was tough for younger kids to succeed. The Class A pitcher I put in was a native Venezuelan and a young pitcher. He pitched four innings and held the other team to no runs but had started getting tired. We didn't know what to do because we had no pitching left. We never thought we could come back from being down so much, so we continued to use the young kid. Our bullpen was depleted, the crowd started getting excited about our comeback and we actually had a shot at winning the game. The other team had a rally going and our manager, Rick Down, who was known as Terre moto (Spanish for Earthquake), asked me to go out and talk to him. I came out of the dugout and the crowd started cheering thinking there would be a pitching change. All the way there I kept thinking about how the crowd would react when they realized we had no one warming up in the bullpen and there was no pitching change in store. I prepared myself for being pelted with trash on my way back. And guess what, as soon as I stepped into the dugout, I got drenched in zambuka, beer and pee combination because the men take a pee in their beer cups instead of going to the bathroom. So there I was, drenched in beer and pee in the eighth inning with the game about to end. As you can see, the fans were very passionate about their ball teams.

VENEZUELA WINTER OF 1991 TO 1992

I was in Venezuela coaching for Aragua when it was announced that the Yankees AAA manager, Buck Showalter was moving up to manage the major league team and he was taking his pitching coach with him. The new AAA manager was going to be Rick Down, the manager I had been working with for the past two years in Venezuela. In my mind, it just seemed logical that I would be his pitching coach in AAA. I would be making my move up the ladder and progressing towards my goal of being a major league pitching coach.

However, I was later told that they were taking the Class A pitching coach to Triple-A while I was to remain with Double-A. This did not sit well with me at all and my world seemed to come crashing down in that instant. I try to look back on that instance with a bit of optimism. The farm director came down to Venezuela to check on the players' progress and I had a meeting with him. I had been passed over for opportunities before and the same thing was repeating itself in coaching. The meeting got heated and I let my temper get the best of me that day. I had one more year left on my contract, but I had pretty much sealed my fate after my confrontation with the farm director. After the 1992 season, I got picked up by the New York Mets after the Yankees let me go. I worked for the Mets until 1997 when I got fired.

1993 TO 1997

I wasn't around my family much, but in the winter of 1992, while having meetings with the Mets, I got a phone call that dad had Alzheimer's Disease. When I came home, I would try spending some nights trying to take care of my dad, but there wasn't much I could do. All three of my brothers were still living together still doing custodial work and helping my mom take care of my dad. My dad passed away early in 1993, just when I was about to join the New York Mets.

Alzheimer's is a terrible disease. I had never seen my dad cry until he finally realized what he was sentenced to. First, was the realization and depression of having the dreaded debilitating disease, and then not knowing that what had usually come easy was now difficult and things that even young kids knew, he no longer knew, and finally, he would know nothing at all.

I remember checking on him while he was in the bathroom one day when he was attempting to spray air freshener in his mouth while thinking it was mouth spray.

Another time when I was spending the night, I was sleeping on the sofa and he woke me up, wide-eyed, and said "Get up off of there"! He said we had to fix the sofa because he had heard the spring popping. And he was not taking no for an answer. He honestly believed there was something terribly wrong with the mattress. At 4 AM in the morning, we had to turn the sofa over to inspect it.

Alzheimer's disease is such an ugly sentence in life.

Mets IN 1997

I was in charge of the pitching staffs for each one of those teams while with the New York Mets. With ten or twelve pitchers on each team, it was my responsibility to train and develop them, especially monitoring their pitching and their pitch limits to ensure their growth.

These were class A teams in 1993 and 1994. In 1995, I did a short season with an A team which was more like a Rookie team in the Appalachian League. This season we won the league championship. Winning is always a great feeling!

In June of 1997, I was fired from the Mets due to the death of a player and some scrambled up damage control on part of the upper management.

I was with the Class A-League in Columbia, South Carolina in early April. It was the start of the season and we were on a road trip to Hagerstown, Maryland. We had gotten snowed out the last game there, so we hopped on the bus to head back to Columbia, an eight to ten-hour drive. Once there, we hopped into our cars and headed back to our apartments. It must have been around midnight and I received a call from the manager that a couple of players were in an accident and one of them had been killed. The next morning, the team was in the locker room with the manager narrating the events of the previous night to everyone.

One of the kids, let's call him F, who was in the accident told us what had happened. Apparently, right before we boarded the bus, the kid who had been killed, A, had snuck in a bottle of vodka in the back of the bus. They were having fun and playing cards. Anyway, F, told us that he asked A if he was alright since he was drinking and had slept on the bus a little after our dinner pit stop. A, responded that he was okay. So, they drove to their apartment via a three-lane interstate. While driving, the car tire blew out, but the car didn't flip and the car stalled smack in the middle of the fast lane of the highway. The kids disembarked and decided to walk towards the shoulder to call for help. They realized that they needed to turn on the car's flashers so that the oncoming traffic would know that the car had stalled. When A went back to turn on the flashers, he saw a car coming toward him in the fast lane, and in panic mode, he jumped the concrete barricade in an attempt to get to safety; only then to be hit by an oncoming vehicle and he was killed.

It was tragic and I told our manager to let the Mets know everything and assumed that it was the end of this terrible incident. However, three days later, due to a neck vertebrae injury requiring surgery, the manager left. A replacement was sent in from Florida, who had no knowledge of this incident. In May, a national newspaper stated that A, the player killed in the accident, had a blood alcohol content of 0.08, which is legally intoxicated.

The Mets top brass came into town to investigate this personally. The farm director, the guy who hired me along with the team psychologist, all came in and interrogated each team member individually.

When it was my turn, they asked me if I knew about A drinking when he was tragically killed. I told them I knew, that everybody knew. I said that I assumed that the manager told them the story. Earlier I had advised the manager to inform them of what had happened and he said that he would. Since he had left the team a couple of days after, I assumed he had contacted the front office. There is a chain of command and the manager of the team is always first in charge.

The Mets did not accept my explanation and decided to let me go, and the entire staff was fired over this incident. The Mets felt that doing so would help do some damage control.

This incident left me bitter at baseball. I didn't want any part of baseball. I sought refuge in my first wife, who I had married in 1995, but her response was to blame me for it. That started making me bitter towards her. The first cracks in our marriage had begun to show.

I was in a very dark place that summer. Baseball was the love of my life and I felt betrayed by the sport and betrayed by the people running the sport. Also, my first wife, instead of helping me through it all, made me even more bitter about the tragic turn of events.

I kept thinking about my future, where was I going to go and what was I going to do next? I would only receive a month's salary and after July, I would have no income, no wages coming in. How would I get by? In order to deal with the financial crunch, I stepped up to giving pitching lessons in Belleville and did some concrete finishing jobs (cement and plasters) through a buddy of mine who got work for me. I would work concrete jobs from seven in the morning to three in the afternoon and then give pitching lessons from four to six in the evening. I was just trying to make a living and soothe my first wife while times were tough, but it was impossible to placate her no matter what I said or did.

I don't remember feeling anxious. I was going to get through this even if it meant doing menial labor until I landed my next job. But my first wife was full of negativity and constantly made me feel like the end of the world was near. I kept reminding her that I would get another job soon enough and that she didn't need to nag me about everything. I was already so bitter about how things were anyway. I definitely did not need to hear more negativity from her

Initially, I thought I was done with baseball for good. The politics of baseball and the betrayal had hurt me deeply. But when I took up those jobs in concrete and pitching lessons, it made me think that I had invested too much in the sport to not leave behind a legacy. I didn't want to be known as the guy who left baseball midway and became a stone mason. That wouldn't be the true me, Dave Jorn and I kept telling myself A big NO to all of this. I knew I had to get back to where I had come from. And, I had definitely come from baseball.

I sent out feelers and resumes in October because that's when most teams are re-evaluating their staffs and looking for new hires. I wound up getting a contract with the Arizona Diamondbacks in the fall of 1997. Things were finally starting to look up for me. I worked for them for three years from 1998 through 2000.

In 1998, I went to Lethbridge, Ontario, with the Diamond-backs in a short-season Class A-League team. The Diamondbacks treated me well and we finished second in the league in 1998 with the team.

In 1999, we didn't have a very good team, but I was with a really solid Christian man, Mike, who helped me with my faith and allowed me to contemplate my relationship with religion and just deeply connect with the Lord. I thank God for him because it was at this time my wife came to visit me in South Bend with a tragic episode for me to hear. She said she had gone out one night and had gotten a ride home with an acquaintance, who had raped her. She said she knew the person and refused to tell me or involve the police in any way at all. I supported her decision at the time but part of me refused to believe that she had been raped. In my heart, I felt that she had been engaged in a consensual relationship in my absence and later on felt guilty about it so she made up a story as to playing the victim in case I ever found out the real truth. She had a strange disposition and she couldn't ever be pleased no matter what I did. She hated her job, hated my job, and also had a drinking problem. Even though initially our marriage started off well, it just fell apart because of her attitude. Even the tiniest things used to bother her.

I remember then I had a good friend named, Brad. He and I were really close. But after my marriage and because my first wife didn't like him I was compelled to cut ties with him. I think back now and believe it was just a bad choice on my part, I shouldn't have let my first wife dominate my friendships. I really tried to please her, but that was a very bad move that I regret to this day.

To this day, I still have not reconnected with Brad. I feel ashamed for how I acted and tossed him and others to the curb. I made some very bad decisions based on a time the Lord was not in my life. I got through that extremely difficult time solely due to Mike, who helped me heal with love and words from the Lord. Now, I truly believe Mike spent lots of time in prayer for me and my many predicaments. Now, I pray that someday I will be able to thank him for his kindness and his prayers.

Again, my career was going well and I was doing what I loved. I even managed the South Bend, Class A team for the Diamondbacks in 2000. But I found out that was not for me. I would much rather coach pitchers than be responsible for the whole team. During that time, my first priority was trying to save my marriage. Even though it probably wasn't savable, I wanted to give it all I had. So I considered scouting for a while where I could work out of my house without having to travel anywhere. With scouting, I would be made responsible to cover a certain area of the United States and create my own schedule, seeing whatever players I needed to see, working on my reports, and also giving time to my marriage at home. I would work a couple of days from home while being on the road the other five days of the week. To me, that seemed more reasonable, because, in minor league baseball, you're gone every day from March through September. There is no coming home and you are forever on the road. That is a huge strain on any marriage, good and bad ones. I knew my first wife couldn't take that. She knew what she was getting into when we got married but somehow she wasn't able to deal with it as graciously as she had imagined. So I was going to opt for scouting for the sake of saving my marriage.

In 2001, I scouted for the New York Yankees and I had Arkansas, Missouri, Kansas, Nebraska, and the Dakotas, which were my areas to scout. Dave Van Horn, my friend, and colleague from back in the 80s was coaching in Nebraska at the time. We both had coached for Coach DeBriyn back in the day and our relationship renewed when I got to Nebraska to scout, I was there a lot because Dave had good players to consider for drafting.

When Dave Van Horn got the job in 2002 at Arkansas as the head coach and succeeding coach DeBriyn, I called him to congratulate him. His response was like, hey, I need a pitching coach, are you tired of the professional ball stuff yet? Come to Arkansas and be my pitching coach.

I told him I needed to discuss it with my wife, although I was ready and willing. When I spoke to her, I asked her what she thought about it. She said that it was my decision to make. The past year, I had given this woman all year of being near me, being at home, and taking a lesser-paying job just for the sake of our marriage and relationship, but she was adamant that she could care less about me or my career or my aspirations in life. I told Dave that I would accept the job and explained to her that I had taken the job, which paid better and was more stable. Her response was a "No" to accompanying me to Arkansas. She told me that it was my decision to make and when she said she wasn't coming with me I told her that was her decision. I knew our marriage was over. I simply could not hold on any longer.

We still tried to hang on to the loose threads that our marriage was dangling on. But Fall of 2002, I came to Arkansas for good. Then in 2003, we got divorced. What was left of our marriage was finally over.

In the 2004 season, our team went to the College World Series. Any other guy in my position would have been on top of the world, but with my personal life having fallen apart, I was just miserable, broken, and emotionally drained. At the time, I didn't want to admit it to myself, but I was running away from the Lord. And when I was miserable, I felt this calling, and I now know the Lord was calling out to me. I couldn't make my mental health and emotional self better in any way I tried! I had this void deep in my soul that refused to go away and no matter what I achieved, how much I earned, or what I purchased, absolutely nothing made me feel good or made my life any better.

I seemed to always run into these men of God randomly around campus. The more I would run away from them, the more they would show up in my vicinity. One of these guys was Josh Folliart. Josh was working for AAO (Arkansas Athlete Outreach), the Christian outreach organization on the campus of the University of Arkansas. He was mentoring our players, having Bible Studies with them, and telling them about Jesus. Every time I turned around, he was there. As much as I needed the Lord in my life, I constantly ran the other way. That is until I could not take it anymore and I was totally broken.

One day, I almost came to blows with our recruiting coordinator and hitting coach, Matt Deggs. Matt and I were very close. He was like my little brother. Later on, when I walked into his office to apologize. I told him I couldn't explain what was happening to me. He suggested that we bring Josh in and discuss it together. All three of us walked into a suite at the ballpark where Josh saw me cry like a baby and on my knees, just broken and sobbing. That's when I begged Jesus to come into my life and suddenly the weight of the world was lifted off my shoulders and, for the next six months, I felt like I was walking around with the Holy Spirit buzzing all around me. In August of 2004, I was born again. Hallelujah, thank you Jesus, and Amen!

Previously, I was a pain to be around, and after I asked the Lord to guide my path, I totally changed as a person. Not that I suddenly became super nice, but an unexplainable peace came over my life, and my heart and the way I looked at things totally changed.

I became almost consumed with the Lord. I would get up every morning, read the Bible, do devotionals and journals which were a learning experience for me since I had previously avoided all religion in my life. I can say that was the year of my rebirth, like a phoenix from the ashes.

I journaled daily and there was this yearly devotional book I maintained. For example, there would be a scripture verse, and I would look it up in the Bible and explore the commentary accompanying the verse to better understand what the Lord was commanding me to do and why I should implement this into my life. Those six months made me experience a different form of love, love of the Lord, and it made me so, so happy. I was absolutely brimming with happiness from within. It was a new feeling for me, an addictive feeling, and definitely a feeling I never wanted to lose ever - Not ever!

I remembered attending Christian Life Cathedral Church and the pastor there, Steve Dixon and his wife Cozy, along with pastor Red, Steve's dad, all were the warmest and most loving people I had ever encountered in my life. That was a time when I was trying to get back on my feet financially since during the divorce proceedings I didn't claim anything, apart from my retirement fund from the time I was with the University of Arkansas and my car. I told my ex-wife to take anything and everything apart from those two things, and she did. This included two homes that both of us were paying towards, a savings account, a checking account, and lots of furniture.

During this time, Coach DeBriyn helped me secure lodgings. I cannot put into words what a wonderful man of God that Norm Debriyn has been to me. He is truly the salt of the Earth. He set me up with Johnny Mike Walker, a big Arkansas baseball booster and fan, who offered me a one-bedroom apartment he owned for $400 a month. It was very tiny. It had a bathroom, kitchen, bedroom, and a small living room. This good fortune and kindness endowed upon me by the Lord helped me to pass through difficult times and get right back on my feet again. The Lord had placed each one of these people into my life for a specific reason and for that I am extremely grateful.

During those times, I also discovered a new sport. Hunting! I had never really hunted before in my life. Growing up, I had baseball, so I never really had the time or inclination to discover other pastimes. I went duck hunting for the first time in my life and then later on I went pheasant hunting with Coach Van Horn, his brother-in-law, and a guy who was an ENT (Ear, Nose, and Throat) surgeon living in Aberdeen, South Dakota.

Pheasant hunting was a fun adventure for me which spurned within me a desire to purchase a gun. I went to the internet and browsed the shotguns I felt would be suitable for hunting. I found one Berretta for around $2500. In my head, I kept hearing this voice telling me I didn't need any gun but then I was being rebellious with myself and ended up purchasing it. Every night, when I got back to my little house, I would scour the internet searching for the best over-under shotgun I could find. I spent night after night researching this and I kept hearing this voice saying "You don't need that" and me saying "Yes, I do, I want it!"

The next morning, I picked up the gun and went to the office to show Coach Van Horn. But in my head, I heard this voice telling me to give the gun away. Give it away! Why should I? But the voice in my head was adamant, I know I had to give the gun away to Red Dixon, a senior pastor at our church. I made a phone call to Christian Life Cathedral Church and asked if I could speak to pastor Red. We spoke and I made an appointment to meet with him a few days later.

I walked up to him on the day of the appointment and told him straight up, "I don't know exactly why I am here, but I am supposed to give you this gun."

He kind of laughed a little at the comment I had just made to him and asked me to be seated. His office had stuffed pheasants all over his walls from when he had hunted in the past. Pheasant hunting was his favorite type of hunting. He mentioned that he had a buddy in California whom he used to hunt with and his friend had passed away not too long ago. He thought his deceased buddy was going to leave him his favorite pheasant hunting gun, but his buddy didn't bequeath him the possession he so ardently desired, a pheasant hunting shotgun.

He told me that I had brought him the exact same shotgun that he had wanted from his friend. All of a sudden, everything clicked and made sense. Since I had never listened to the Holy Spirit from the very beginning, that gun actually belonged to pastor Red. This incident occurred in early 2005.

When I tell people this story, they look at me like I am a little bit crazy, because they don't understand the background behind it all. How I'd found the Lord and how he guided me to do what I did. I guess personal context and your own personal relationship with the Lord matters a lot in situations.

Red was a lot like a father to me during, before, and after the shotgun incident. During one of his Sunday sermons, which I remember quite vividly, I would like to share here. Red said it is possible that you are the pilot of your own airplane and if you run into a storm, and the instruments on the plane ceased to work, he asked what we should do in that situation? The obvious answer was to get out of the storm quickly so we can get the plane up and running again. And his analogy was that storms come into our lives, not to destroy us, but to help us to become stronger and save us if we act accordingly. The key is to not give up and not put our heads down, but to brave the storms of our lives. That's a lesson I carry with me every single day of my life. And, I pray and put my trust in the Lord to lead me and deliver me through every single situation.

During those times, I also built up enough tolerance within me to forgive my ex-wife. I even sent her a couple of books and CDs about the Lord, hoping it could have some sort of impact on her regardless of how bitter our marriage and subsequent divorce had turned out.

I had a hard time disciplining the players as a coach in those days, but everything else was pretty much a walk down an easy street for me as I walked every day of my life alongside my Lord and Savior, Jesus Christ. I was softer towards my players and more approachable, but I never let my competitive streak wane or the work ethic that was instilled in me from the start, because I knew we had to work hard to be the very best.

I survived all the turmoil in my life due to the Lord and His blessings in my life. Finding Him helped me to recognize just how merciful the Lord had been to me. I had all this animosity I had harbored within me regarding my childhood, my upbringing, my financial adversity, and having bad luck in baseball opportunities. But after accepting the Lord in my life, I learned to forgive and let go of all of the feelings of hatred that I had harbored in my heart for so many years. My heart and soul are fully encircled in forgiveness. And, I totally have my Lord and Savior, Jesus Christ, to thank for everything that happened and changed in my life.

Matt Deggs left us not long after my rebirth. He was hired by Texas A&M. There, he wasn't accountable for all of his baseball decisions and he started having issues with alcohol. I tried to help him quit because alcohol was ruining his life. He lost his job at A&M and nearly lost his family and his life. Everything nearly fell apart before it fell back into place for him again. He is now head baseball Coach at Louisiana University. And he is also a Christian motivational speaker. We text each other routinely and have never lost touch to date. My life has been truly blessed by sticking beside my friend, Matt, and praying for and encouraging him.

I think of Josh Foliart a lot now, he was the reason I started attending Christian Life Cathedral Church. He has started a church or two in Peru and is involved in doing some leadership work as well. I last saw him a couple of years ago, and then the COVID-19 pandemic hit created distances so we didn't get a chance to catch up. Looking back on our friendship, I see the Lord put Josh into my life to witness to me and prepare me for salvation. And he eventually introduced me to my second wife, Melinda.

KYLE ATKINS:

There is another young man and former Razorback baseball player who attended Christian Life Cathedral Church, known as Kyle Atkins. He was an outfielder for us and I had nicknamed him, "Rev", because he would always be preaching in the locker room and before practice. Kyle and I would always discuss the Lord and what I had read that day. We would discuss a scripture verse and just live in that day's moment of spirituality. He was kind of carrying forward Josh's legacy, maintaining the decorum of preaching the Lord's words.

Late in the year 2005, I purchased a four-bedroom and two-bath house off of Porter Road in Fayetteville, Arkansas. It was only possible because I managed to save a lot while living in that small apartment for $400 a month. This was before I married my wife, Melinda. After marriage, I sold that and bought one in Polo Estates out in Goshen, Arkansas, which is right outside of the Fayetteville city limits.

Our team was blessed in 2009 when the Razorbacks went to the College World Series. And, again in the years 2012 and 2015.

2016 wasn't that good a year for us, but I knew the players were doing all they could. There were five or six freshmen pitchers and they just weren't ready for what was expected of them on the field.

During those years, I would be conducting chapel service on Sundays for the kids at home and on the road. I would be feeling something and I would look it up in the Bible and deliver a sermon based on that. Similarly, on religious holidays such as Easter, I would look up the history and the significance and deliver sermons on that and what we can learn from this Holy Day. I would invite all pitchers to my room on a Sunday before we embarked on the bus and I would discuss the Lord in detail. Even though we were unable to perform well on the field, these sermons made me feel what the Lord wanted me to feel that I was being used by him.

I was performing for the Lord and He wanted me to spread His message.

Also, I would organize the chapel service with other speakers such as pastor Red Dixon and Evangelist, Ron Harris. Whomever I could get to come over and speak about the Lord and offer the kids a fresh and new perspective about the Lord and His saving grace, I would ask to come to speak to our players.

In 2016, my last year as pitching coach for the Razorbacks was the least productive year on the field, but my most productive year off the field. The Lord used me to make a difference in kids' lives, especially in my freshman pitchers of 2016. Because those boys became the men of 2018 and nearly won the National College Baseball Championship. I was so proud of them.

I retired in 2016 and I scout part-time for the Tampa Bay Rays. Now, I am helping two area scouts in Arkansas, Missouri, Kansas, and Oklahoma. Both of these scouts have large areas. Whenever they have a conflict of being at two places at the same time I cover for them, which often happens. At the beginning of the week, the Rays will let me know where I am going and who I need to evaluate. Predominantly, I go to four-year schools within about a 5 hour radius from home. Occasionally I see some junior college players and high school players. I am blessed to still be involved in the game I love. From mid-February to the end of

June, I am typically somewhere watching a weekend series, Friday through Sunday.

My idea or philosophy of training starts with routine things you do every day, such as jogging to get warm, flexibility, and playing catch first to warm up. Flexibility is extremely important for an athlete. If your hamstrings are tight, you must work on those and if you are stiff in the hips, you need to work on that to build a range of motion in your body. When you play catch it's not just about getting loose, but working on accuracy mechanics, and arm strength. We play with one ball. If it's thrown wildly, you go get it and learn the importance of control. You have to invest your entire body and mind in the daily routine and need to be in pristine condition before you can consider yourself ready for the game. It's always the little things that are important

I would sometimes make my players run up and down hills 'like Cleveland Hill. I would force them to get up early in the morning to do runs. There would be days when they would whine and complain but I would keep pushing - because that's what makes winners. You don't feel like getting up and playing? Your muscles are sore? I always strived for my players to develop a guilty attitude in themselves if they failed to do the work expected of them. You see it's easy to say "I don't feel like doing it today". Then, that becomes easy to say the same thing again tomorrow. I wanted to trust them to do what they had to do because they would feel guilty if they didn't. Guilty to letting themselves and their teammates down. You see, "Quitters never win and winners never quit". We had games to win and people to impress with our skills. That is also where the mental conditioning comes in. I have mentioned earlier that even if you are at par with your competitors in terms of physical skills, what decides who wins is mental strength.

This reminds me of a story that my wife, Melinda told me several years ago about her developing toughness in her own life. In the hot summer of the year before going into the 5th grade, she got a summer job picking tomatoes at her neighbor's tomato farm. Melinda would set her alarm for 5:30 am, rise when the alarm went off, get dressed, and head to the tomato patch. Arriving about the same time the sun came up, she'd grab an empty bushel basket and pick tomatoes until the basket was full. She would drag the bushel to the end of the dirt-filled row, grab an empty basket and repeat this over and over until she and the other workers would finish picking every tomato vine in the field. Sweaty and dirty, she would head home, shower, have lunch, and hit the sack by 8:30 pm each night. This was in Arkansas and the temperatures reached the middle to the upper 90s every day. Melinda did this for 5 consecutive summers and her parents allowed her to save the money she had earned. Eventually, she used this hard earned money along with what she earned from other summer jobs to pay for ALL her spending money during her 4 years of college. She learned mental and physical strength and toughness and this is exactly what I wanted my players to learn to be able to be the best they could be.

Also, I am going to share another story that some of my former pitchers will probably remember for the rest of their lives. "Cleveland Hill" is all you would need to say to my pitchers and they would immediately have a mental video show up in their minds. The video would show Cleveland Hill, the tallest and steepest incline of any hill in Fayetteville, Arkansas. To develop mental and physical strength, we would get in our vehicles and drive to the "hill". After getting out of their cars, the pitchers would go to the bottom of the hill and would begin their trek up and down Cleveland Hill. They ran this once a week for a month.

This definitely developed mental and physical toughness in them that they dug down deep in times of extreme difficulties in baseball games and were able to finish the task which without the "hill" experience, they would not have been tough enough to finish successfully. Hopefully, they have used this experience many times in their everyday lives after baseball, because we all know that life isn't easy. Whoever has built in his mind a strong fortress can turn even a lost game in his favor and into a win. So when I would force my players to do things they didn't want to do, which their bodies wouldn't allow them to do, I was in essence preparing them to train their minds to make tough calls for the sake of the team, for the sake of winning and for toughness for the rest of their lives! On the field, in a game, the pressure is immense, you have your competitors, you have your fans screaming all around you, and you have the weight of expectations on your shoulders of friends, families, coaches, school, and the team. Only those aptly trained in mental toughness can bear the brunt of all of this stress. My question is "Are we adequately preparing our youth for the stress of living in the tough times they are put in today?" We may need to rethink the way we are raising the youth of today!?! Could this mental weakness be what is causing many of today's tragedies in America?

I always taught my players that I needed to be able to trust them. I couldn't babysit them 24/7 and at the same time I needed to be able to know they were putting in the relevant efforts and doing things the right way, so I would tell them never to lie to me because eventually they would get found out and then the trust would be broken and they sure as heck wouldn't want me breathing down their necks micromanaging them. Because once trust is broken it is hard to gain it back. And sadly, the truth is that "one lie usually leads to many others!"

When people wonder how I instill competitiveness in my players, I tell them that winning is addictive. Once you get a taste of the recognition and thrill it brings from being the best in the game, you get hooked on it and never want to let go of the adrenaline rush that spurs from it. The tougher the training, the more difficult it becomes for the players to give up easily. The training embeds within them this work ethic, competitiveness and consistency which then gives rise to confidence. And everything just escalates from there. The key is to get the players to make small consistent efforts from day to day and always have the mindset of a winner like *I can win this, I can beat that team,* and on and on. I really tried hard to toughen my guys up through conditioning, which was really difficult.

As a coach, we are paid to win. And believe me, no one wants to win more than me. But I never let winning consume me. My personal philosophy was about preparation taking care of wins. I put my guys through the torture of practice so that the games were a piece of cake. It was all about how you prepared, how you worked, and how you competed. If you checked all the boxes, then win or lose you were a winner to me and I could respect and live with the losses.

I remember once in the 1985 team, things had started to get a little lax and I had to give my pitchers a wake-up call. We had just gotten boat raced, pummeled 16-2 in five innings by Mississippi State. The game was called in the 5th inning with them still hitting. They were loaded that year and they had four future MLB all-stars on their team. Jeff Brantley, Rafael Palmero, Will Clark, and Bobby Thigpen are the four guys that I am talking about. I felt we were getting complacent. We had a very,

very good team as well. So the next day, May 1st, we played them again at Ray Winder Field in Little Rock. I decided that I needed to turn up the intensity and challenged them with some running sprints and lots of them, including our starting pitcher. Coach Debriyn initially thought I had lost my mind, but I knew they all could handle it. Our starter, Fred Farwell, later that same day, went eight innings and we beat them 13-1. We never lost another game in May, our record was 17-0, and on to Omaha, Nebraska, to compete in the College World Series.

Also, I used to always consider what each player might be going through in his personal life, because that has a profound impact on your mental strength. You have to counsel them and encourage them because as a coach your only responsibility does not lie in pushing them physically. You have to build a rapport and ensure the players' emotional stability prevails game after game after game. Similarly, if the player starts coming under some form of superiority complex, you have to give him a wake-up call so he doesn't slough off. True timing and the situation matters a lot in what kind of personality trait I needed to build for the player in question. I was expected and needed to be a leader, a motivator, a father figure, a friend, and a shoulder to cry on. Being a coach encompassed all that for me and so much more and it's something I am incredibly proud of.

My time in coaching had been one heck of a ride.

Throughout my life, I have always had the desire to be great and to do my best. I believe that God placed this in my heart and I had to accept it, work hard for it, and mature into it. Through my school, career, marriages, and life, God has always been there watching over me, and I clearly see that now looking back. I am so grateful that He has been so kind to me and now I want to encourage others to open their hearts to what God has for them. More important than teaching my players how to develop mental and physical toughness was God's calling on me to teach them about Jesus and lead them to a spirit-filled life with Him.

One example of this involved an extremely gifted pitcher that everyone figured would be drafted in the first round of the professional draft. He was big and strong, threw hard and accurately, and was deceivingly left-handed. This meant most batters couldn't tell what he was going to pitch to them and most would end up striking out on the pitches that he sent their way. This certain young man was one of my wife, Melinda's favorite boys. She loved and bragged, mothered, and doted on all of them, but she and this young man just hit it off from the first time they met. She and I are both aware that this was our Lord and Savior, Jesus, working a mother/son type relationship between them that would ready this young man for what was about to happen to his life. Just when everything in his life was almost perfect and he felt as if he was on top of the world, things started falling apart. First, he was dating a beautiful Christian girl who was also a student at the University of Arkansas. She came to all of his games and they were practically inseparable. After a few months of dating, she realized she was pregnant with his child. He came to me and talked to me about the situation he was in. I prayed with him and encouraged him that all things would work out. He needed to be a man in this situation and support her through this time too. I had shared his situation with my wife and we prayed for both of them. The next Sunday afternoon, he was one of a few pitchers that I had called to the field to work with in the bullpen. While working with the other guys, Melinda asked him to come to my office to talk to him. During their conversation, she led him to accept Jesus as his Lord and Savior, which was a total life changer for him and his life.

A few weeks later, my wife and I stood up for him and his girlfriend as they were married.

Later on in professional baseball, as he indeed was drafted in the 1st round, he experienced a serious injury that would end his pitching career. Without his strong relationship with Jesus, and prayers from friends and family members, I truly don't know how he would have survived all of these life-changing events that had taken place in his life. To this day, this young man continues to follow the Lord and has put Him first in his life. He is a loving husband, father, and friend to many. Thank you, Lord, for putting this young man in my life and for blessing me to be a part of him coming to know the Lord, and for being able to live a happy, blessed, and successful life.

STORIES

STORY ONE: THE CHOSEN ONE

The story I'm about to tell has been narrated to me by my mom. While visiting my maternal grandparents in Belleville, mom was changing my diaper. Back in the '50s, you had these cloth diapers and they would be soiled, washed, dried, and reused. These diapers were tied together with a safety pin. So, as the story goes, mom had this safety pin in her mouth as she was dealing with a wiggly six months old me, and trying hard to tie the diaper in place. Suddenly, she says something, and the safety pin falls from her mouth directly into mine and everyone is in panic mode! My grandpa is trying to shake it out of me, but good heavens I have already swallowed it! I am rushed to the hospital where they gave me some laxatives and instructions to look for that safety pin in my diapers. If by any twist of fate, it doesn't appear, they would need to remove it surgically. The first two days, nothing happened. Then suddenly, when it was looking like we would have to go into surgery, the pin turns up nice and easy into my diaper, still wide open. It was a miracle that it never got stuck in anything and made a clean exit. When I think back to this story, it makes it feel like the Lord foretold my future and our family that I was meant for great things and His blessings would follow me all the way.

STORY TWO: THE BASEBALL GLOVE

For hours and hours at home, I would be throwing a rubber ball or bouncing it off the walls while replaying the St. Louis Cardinal line-up in my head. I would go out with my friends and be bouncing a ball in the air. It was amazing being outside just playing ball. I simply loved playing baseball and practically lived with a baseball in my hand. When it would be too cold outside, I would be in the basement throwing balls around, breaking light bulbs, and barely avoiding trouble with my parents. We weren't exactly living the good life, but my mind keeps playing back to this one time when I was sitting on a couch at home. The couch's arm was ripped, and the white batting was falling out of it, and there I am wearing a worn-out baseball glove with the webbing busting out of it. But I am happy. I am as happy as I could ever be because I had my trusty ball and glove with me. What more out of life did I need.

STORY THREE: WHAT DOESN'T ACTUALLY KILL YOU, ACTUALLY MAKES YOU STRONGER

In elementary school, we had this one nun who would always pull our ears for punishment and I even tried complaining to my dad about it. However, dad insisted that no matter what, she could pull my ears because I probably deserved it. Similarly, in my junior year at high school, even though I made the basketball team, we weren't good that year. Our coach would divide 12 of us into six groups of two each, facing each other. He would roll the ball on the floor, and call out a group number. That group would dive onto the floor and fight for the loose ball. After about 30 minutes of this, the coach lined us up under the basket and sprayed an alcohol spray on our floor burns. You just gritted your teeth and took it. Those were different times indeed, but it makes me think, that it didn't kill us - instead, it made us stronger. He probably should have figured out a better way to make us stronger, but it was what it was.

STORY FOUR: FIRST TIME TRAVELLING

The following story happened in my freshman year of junior college, and the year is 1972. We were playing against the University of Illinois Junior Varsity Team and had to go to Champaign, Illinois, to play them. This was my first time to ever travel. I don't even remember seeing the ocean before I was 21 years old because we just never went anywhere. I mean, I used to live 20 miles from St. Louis and even that seemed like another country to me, so you can imagine my excitement when we had to go outside our town to play.

We were playing two games, one each day, and after the first game, we went back to the hotel to shower and change. The bus was to take us to eat and would pick us up in a few hours. Well after eating, we went and had a few beers, because the drinking age was 18 at that time. When we all got on the bus one of our players who had come out of the game with a pulled hamstring, got on and was feeling pretty buzzed, so he felt no pain and was walking normally. Coach was livid! We had lost the game, a kid gets hurt in the game and now he's feeling no pain and most of his team is buzzed. So when we got back to the hotel, he has us line up for some sprints. We ran and ran and ran with guys throwing up. But we all had a tough lesson in learning how to act when you lose.

STORY FIVE: THE REBEL

Back when I was in elementary school, my mom would send me to the Snyder Store to get groceries. That was the only store in Shiloh and other than the grocery store, we only had a tavern in our town. The owner, Vernon Snyder, would walk me across the street safely. That would make me so mad. I would go back across the street alone and then come back across alone just because I was a rebel.. Similarly, dad would send me with 25 cents to grab a bucket of beer from the tavern for him to drink. I would almost always test out the beer myself, despite being barely eight years old. Boy, how life and times have changed!

STORY SIX: MEETING MELINDA

My wife was born and raised in Van Buren and spent most of her life there apart from attending the University in Arkansas for her undergraduate degree. She became an elementary school teacher and retired in 2017. She has 35 years of teaching experience which includes grades between Kindergarten to 5th grade. Also, she taught adjunct for the University of Arkansas in Ft. Smith and in Fayetteville during her 35 years in education. After we got married she and Maggie, her daughter, moved to Fayetteville and she taught third grade at Root Elementary. Her oldest daughter was in Oxford, Mississippi, going to Ole Miss.

In the summer of 2002, I came to Arkansas without my ex-wife. She never came with me and our marriage was falling apart bit by bit until she asked for a divorce. My divorce was finalized towards the end of 2003 and I was devastated. Nothing ever worked out for me. I went through the whole year of 2004 bitter and devoid of any feelings whatsoever. Josh Folliart was ministering to the baseball team, through AAO (Arkansas Athlete Outreach). The AAO was basically the religious element of the university's athletic department. They used to do mentoring and counseling and spread the word of the Lord on campus. They were the ones spreading the gospel.

At the time, I felt incredibly threatened by Josh. It was 2004 and the world was a terrible place for me at the time. Josh would always be around and if I would see him coming one way, I would turn around and practically run the other way. In August 2004, I was a hopelessly broken man and I just called out to Josh and accepted Christ for the third time in my life. I had always felt a void in my life. This time though it really took hold of my heart and I felt the Lord's timing was just perfect. Josh and I grew really close and my heart was on fire for the Lord.

So, Josh happened to be in Melinda's adjunct class at U of A Fort Smith (She had her master's degree and taught college-level classes to make extra money). Josh mentioned me to Melinda, and her being an unbelievable Christian, asked Josh about my relationship with Christ. He told her that I was a good, strong Christian man who journals and also spreads the word of the Gospel. I am sure if I wasn't that way, Melinda wouldn't have had anything to do with me.

Melinda, at first, was hesitant to meet me, but her mom convinced her that it would be harmless to meet me. She had been divorced a few years and I sounded similar to her in beliefs and passion for Christ. Melinda had two daughters and was living with her mother in Van Buren. The oldest, Molly, was in college, whereas the younger one, Maggie, was in the sixth grade.

Josh decided to set me up on a blind date with Melinda. Tagging along was Josh, Josh's wife Cassandra, Trey Holloway (one of my pitchers), and his future wife Kristin. We met at Noodles restaurant in Fayetteville. We hit it off instantly and there was both a spiritual and mental connection between us. We just talked and talked and talked and it all came naturally. Just like that, we started dating. She was teaching in Van Buren and I was coaching in Fayetteville at the U of A and we would try to coordinate and get together as often as we could.

The more we met and spent time together, the more we knew we couldn't live without each other, and "us" was a together going to be a forever concept. But, she told me she had Multiple Sclerosis (MS), and initially, it didn't affect me. However, as time passed, I started getting more and more worried about our future together and what would happen to her as we both aged with her MS diagnosis.

One time, in the summer of 2006, she was coming back from Oxford, Mississippi, where Molly went to college and I had been recruiting in Little Rock.

Little Rock was on the way to Van Buren and we had decided to have dinner after I was done with the games and she would drive back to Van Buren afterward. When she called to confirm our date, I made a lame excuse that I wouldn't be able to make it to dinner because I had to watch some extra games, I didn't sound very convincing at all and she could see right through it. I could sense her disappointment over the phone but she didn't push it. However, after giving it some thought, I called her back and said that I would skip the games and we could still make it to our dinner date. We met at the restaurant and she straight up told me to my face, "I don't know what is up with you, Dave, but you need to make up your mind because I don't have time for all this indecisive stuff. Either you're all in or I'm OUT!"

I was a little taken back by the bluntness of it all, even though I was the one with the commitment issues. I told her I was scared about her MS and where it would lead us in the future. For me, it was like a thirsty man finding an oasis at the brink of dehydration, only to find out it was a mirage after a few imaginary sips of water because of her MS diagnosis.

She only had one answer to all my inhibitions. It is what it is and I needed to figure out what I wanted to do with us. The thought of losing her, not to MS, but to my stupidity, was impossible to bear. I knew I loved her and my fears shouldn't matter between us. So, at Christmas time, I proposed. And in April of 2007, we were married.

Our wedding is also a funny story. We were together at her mom's house, me, Melinda, the girls, her brother, and mom when I proposed. We decided to get married in June or July after the baseball season was over. Randomly, on the road to the University of Tennessee, I said to myself, why must we wait at all? It's not like we haven't been married before and we need a grand wedding or anything. So I called Melinda to ask her what she thought about getting married right now, and she was all in!

So we got married during the baseball season on April 6th, 2007, right before a Friday night game! We had a small wedding service at our church. We had a family lunch and I went to our game. We spent our wedding night at the Embassy Suites and I went to work the next day.

We have been married 15 years as of this April 2022. When we got married, I was coaching at Arkansas and Melinda was finishing teaching her school year in Van Buren while Maggie wrapped up her school year alongside her mom. And Molly was at "Old Mississippi" I'm not a fan of them so I refuse to call them "Ole Miss". We were looking for a bigger house to move into and ended up buying a house in Polo Estates in Goshen, right out of Fayetteville. Maggie and Melinda joined me in the summer after the school year ended. Maggie went to Woodland Junior High in Fayetteville in the Fall and Melinda got a teaching job at Root Elementary. Molly, our oldest daughter, had started college at the University of Mississippi, our arch-rival in baseball. She had worked hard in school and got a scholarship, which paid her tuition in school.

Our youngest daughter, Maggie, now lives in New York and is engaged to Chris Verrillo. Chris is a fine, hard-working young man who loves Maggie and will be a loving husband to her.

Molly is married to Kaleb Kuhl, a strong man of God. They have 3 beautiful sons.

Throughout my marriage, Melinda has been my rock. Since I would be around the guys all day long, screaming and charging full speed ahead and being constantly competitive, it was a difficult adjustment to mellow my tone at home. Melinda softened me up for it and I could easily transition into my role as a husband and stepfather with more ease.

Melinda's spirituality and her faith in Jesus through fervent prayer really pulls us through whatever life throws our way. I sometimes joke that she has a personal hotline to the Lord. She is a prayer warrior with nothing but love in her heart. While living in Fayetteville, every time we would go out, we would run into Melinda's students or parents of former students and they would all be so excited to see her. It would always be like Mrs. Jorn, you were our favorite teacher and it's all because her heart was so pure. She has unlimited love for everyone, especially kids. Melinda is 62 years old now and was 28 when she was diagnosed with MS. Although the diagnosis was devastating and scary for her, she heard a quiet whisper from the Lord telling her that everything was going to be okay. And she trusted that. She trusted in the Lord to get her through everything and He has. Most people with MS usually atrophy away, but my warrior, Melinda, is much stronger. Apart from being weak on her left side and being unable to stand the heat and humidity, she is pretty normal. She has faith in God and trusts that He will take care of her, and he does. She has a heart for winning souls for the Lord and she follows this lead every opportunity she gets. She has a beautiful heart and a beautiful soul.

Another story that I wish to narrate regarding my better half is after her retirement in 2017, Melinda signed up to drive for Uber. We don't live very far from the Airport in Bentonville, so she would do airport pick-ups and drops offs.

People would always talk to her because Melinda just radiates this love vibration wherever she goes. She would always talk about the Lord during her Uber trips and one time she had a guy accept Christ while she was Ubering him to his destination. So, that's my Melinda for you, folks. I know her neurologist, and he told me that she was so persistent with witnessing to him and providing him tracks that he eventually ended up surrendering to the Lord and accepting Christ.

I kept thinking back to my previous life whenever I think about my marriage to Melinda. Had she entered my life prior to 2004, we wouldn't ever have clicked or fallen in love. A few years earlier we both were poles apart. So, it all makes me feel that everything was meant to be this way. I was meant to hit rock bottom before I could accept Christ and before I met Melinda.

STORY SEVEN: CARACAS, VENEZUELA, WINTER 1990:

Coaching winter ball in Venezuela was a whole different environment. This one time, when we were getting ready for the game and I was walking down to the bullpen with my starting pitcher, the military police were there with their guns and German shepherds, and all were lined up at the outfield wall. I was a little nervous at the moment because you never knew what was going to happen there. One of the cops just let his dog jump at me and pulled him back just in time to scare me. I jumped back while he was laughing his butt off for getting me on that one.

STORY EIGHT: SH*T

We were playing in Caracas back in the winter of 1991, and Caracas is located right in the mountains with the sky and clouds all around it. It looked like it was going to pour down rain as the clouds were gathering and were intensely dark, but we were still preparing for batting practice. I was playing catch out in front of the dugout, with a native Venezuelan coach. I felt something hard and wet hit my shoulder and I thought that it had started to rain. I told the Venezuelan coach that I had felt some rain. In my weak Spanish, I said "lluvia" and pointed to my shoulder. He responded in his broken English, "No lluvia, shit"! A pigeon had pooped on my shoulder. We both had a good laugh on that one.

STORY NINE: WE ARE LOST IN THE MIDDLE OF NOWHERE

In the summer of 1988, when I was contemplating returning to professional ball, I got a job for the summer with the Cardinals Rookie Ball team in Johnson City, Tennessee. We were heading to Burlington, North Carolina. When we got on the bus, I noticed that the driver was wearing those thick coke bottle glasses and wearing hearing aids. I sat directly behind the bus driver and the manager sat to the right.

We were on an overnight trip to Burlington, North Carolina. After the last game, we returned to Johnson City. We packed up the bus and headed for home, only I felt like we were going the wrong way. I attempted to ask the "bussie," what the driver is called, if we are going the right way. He doesn't hear me, so I tap him on the shoulder and ask him. He says "This is the direction they gave me at the ballpark". Now, I am thinking to myself that you just drove here a day ago, so why do you need to get directions? So I let it go, but still think we are headed in the opposite direction of Johnson City. Now, we are about one hour down the road and I see a sign for Durham, North Carolina, and now I know for sure that we are definitely going the wrong way. I see a rest area ahead and told him to pull in and get new directions. Sure enough, we were an hour in the wrong direction. So, it's another hour back to where we started. Now two whole hours on the road and we'd gone nowhere! To make matters worse he got confused and starts to get back on the interstate heading the wrong way again. So, I get him to pull into a gas station for a map. I get us back on track to Johnson City. It's now around 3 a.m. and we are on the interstate to Johnson City. A straight shot, and practically no way the driver could mess it up. I am tired and decide to lie down, close my eyes, and rest. No sooner than I lie down and I hear him downshift and he's pulling off the highway. He shuts the bus off, turns to me, and says "This is the funniest thing, I think we've run out of gas". By now the players are getting all over this poor little old man. The confused driver makes a call to the bus company and they send another bus for us. By the time we get back home, it's 11 a.m. A four-hour trip suddenly turned into an eleven-hour one.

STORY TEN: CRAZY FANS

Mazatlan, Mexico, in 1980, and this was my first experience with winter ball. It was a strange place to be because I didn't speak the language and they had chicken wire all around the ballpark because the crowd would just throw stuff at you. One time, there wasn't a bullpen in our field and the pitcher would just mark sixty feet and six inches from the dugout, where he would place a towel. This is where he would begin warming up with the catcher. The crowd started throwing firecrackers at the catcher when he was about to catch the ball. The people only did this to watch him jump in fear. Smoke bombs were routinely thrown into the dugout. This was routine and things were just totally out of control! Thank goodness Mazatlan was on the Pacific Coast and next to the beach. We were off on Mondays, so I would always end up at the ocean every Monday, able to relax and get my mind off of those crazy fans at the ballpark.

Similarly, once we a played game in Culiacan, the drug capital of Mexico, and there were twenty thousand fans in the stadium. We would wait after the end of each game for the stands to get cleared so we could depart, but this one time, the fans just refused to leave. We had to make our way to the bus through the crazy crowds, lines of people on both sides yelling and screaming. As soon as we hopped on the bus and the driver turned on the ignition, a two-by-four just rammed into our windshield, and rocks were thrown at the bus. I was on the bus floor while the bus just drove away like it was nothing. I finally figured out the fans didn't like us beating them that day. Nuts!

Also, there were always fights between innings amongst the fans because they would be drinking beer and getting drunk. I once saw a policeman pin down a drunken fan on the stadium steps, only to have him wrestle his weapon from him and I ducked for fear it would go off. The other police rammed him in the head with the butt of his gun and drug him away before he caused any more problems. The men rarely will go to the bathroom. They take a pee in their beer cups and any game-ending celebration begins with them throwing the pee cups in the air. Thank heavens they had installed chicken wire there or else the players would have to deal with a lot of trash thrown their way!

Those were definitely some crazy times and I will NEVER forget them either!

STORY ELEVEN: RAY AND BILL

Ray Harris was one of the pitchers that I coached at the University of Arkansas. He always had a difficult time with the toughness of our conditioning. I was incredibly tough on my kids since I wanted them to be the best and Ray had decided he would just quit. So, he happened to call home his freshman year and tell his mom that he couldn't take it anymore and that his pitching coach (me) was a slave driver and he just wanted to return home. His mom put his dad on the phone, who told him simply to suck it up and stay! When he told me this story, I was all up in stitches with laughter. Yeah, I was a tough boss, but come on, it was for their own good. They were just too immature to realize it at the time.

Later on, Ray told me all of the players were really grateful they had me as a coach. Despite my tough attitude, when all the results were in and we had made it to the College World Series, they knew they wouldn't have wanted anyone else to coach them.

There was another kid I coached, his name was Bill Gunger. He wasn't a pitcher but an outfielder. He credits me for his life success because he now owns a company worth millions of dollars and resides in Raleigh, North Carolina. Even though he didn't have much of a baseball career, he still feels he owes me for whatever discipline and principles I instilled in him during his baseball career at the University of Arkansas.

STORY TWELVE: BASEBALL CHAPEL

Growing up Catholic, I knew there was a God, I just didn't know how to access him! I didn't have any relationship with the

Lord. I often used to search for meaning in life beyond baseball. I had this deep void in my heart and I didn't know how to fill it.

I knew what was right and wrong, but I didn't know how to fill this space in my heart. There was Baseball Chapel Service prior to games on Sundays in pro ball. They had a pastor who would lead prayers on Sundays and do a short version of church. With day games on Sunday, there was no time to go to church.

I first became aware of the chapel concept in 1977 in Gastonia, North Carolina. And I really wanted to be a part of it. I attended service and would always feel better. Also, I always felt that this was what I really needed.

However, at the same time, I was too busy chasing girls and partying to let spirituality properly take over. I still remembered in 1980, I was on this long bus ride while playing in Little Rock and I just felt so alone and so lost. But perhaps I wasn't ready for it at that time because the feelings never properly took hold. I do know now that the Lord always had a plan for me because he looked out for me all along. Sometimes, I think perhaps I wasn't mature enough at the time to let the Lord help me turn my life around. The devil would have me believe that I would need to undergo this major transformation to fully accept the Lord, which would mean giving up lots of vices that I had come to enjoy and own as part of my life. I wasn't ready to face difficulties in this regard. I felt this was all too much fun and I deserved it. But no matter what I did, even at the prime of my partying lifestyle, it never did help fill the void I harbored in my heart. The Lord came through for me eventually when I was ready. Yet again I felt that these things happen in the Lord's perfect timing.

STORY THIRTEEN: GETTING PETS

My youngest stepdaughter, Maggie, has this undeniable love of pets. My oldest stepdaughter Molly, felt the same about animals. At the time Maggie was in junior high, she kept asking me to get her a dog and I just kept saying no. Then one day I just gave in and decided to take the girls to the pet store to browse. We picked up this little furball and took him to the playpen to play with. When we decided to leave, he just started yelping and I went all soft and mushy. I agreed to take him home with us. At the same time my oldest daughter, Molly, had picked out a female of the same breed that she really liked. So, we ended up taking both of them home. Maggie named the male, Duggar, after her favorite player, Jake Duggar, on our baseball team. And the female was named Daisy, by Molly. They were both a mix of a poodle and Bichon Frise. Both girls loved the dogs but Duggar became their favorite because of his playful nature. On the way home, we went to a neighborhood market and we ran into Jake Duggar who was out with his girlfriend. I told him one of the pups was named Duggar after him. Oh my gosh, Maggie would have killed me in that moment if she could have, but it was funny.

We ended up putting Daisy down in 2017 and Duggar in 2018. Daisy had Cushing's disease, which was painful and she lost all use of her back legs. Her hair had started falling out and she was in doggy diapers. We had to put her down since we couldn't bear her anguish. Duggar had neared the end of his life and he was eventually put to sleep in 2018.

STORY FOURTEEN: FATHER-DAUGHTER BOND

I don't have any biological children of my own. My only kids are my stepdaughters. My stepdaughter from my first wife was in junior high back when we got married. We had a good relationship and I helped her in different areas of her life. Christina has two children, twins, Kellan and Alexis. It's amazing how the Lord can always use a bad situation for good.

Remarrying, I was closer to Maggie because Molly was in college and never home very much. With Maggie, I would be packing her lunches and taking her to school, so we grew really close. I think my relationship with the Lord helped my relationship with my kids. Like Maggie wanting to get those dogs, I remembered telling her time and again that keeping pets is a big responsibility and she would have to take care of them. But then in the mornings, I couldn't bear to wake her up early to feed the dogs so I would end up doing it myself. My spirituality had made me really mushy and my girls were just such a blessing in my life that I would always back down to whatever they wanted or needed. I spoiled them tremendously, which sometimes isn't a good thing, but I had moved beyond being a person who ignites conflict and to someone more at peace just agreeing to my girl's wishes although I continued enforcing how they must learn responsibility.

Not to say that we didn't have our conflicts. Because we did. In high school, I had set the bar high that Maggie was supposed to get a 3.5 GPA in her last high school semester to go to college. When she was getting ready to go to college, we got our hands on her report card and it wasn't what it was supposed to be. She was such a smart kid, but she didn't apply herself and I was disappointed. I told her I wouldn't pay for her college and she was to live at home because she knew the consequences of not studying hard enough. She got really mad and went to live with her father in Van Buren.

We are okay now. Ups and downs are part of a father-daughter relationship. Doesn't change the love I have for my girls one little bit. Our oldest daughter, Molly, went out of state to college her first year and returned to the University of Arkansas to complete her last three years of college. During those three years, Molly and I became much closer and were able to spend more time together. Both girls were well respected and beautiful young ladies. Two sisters could not look any more different than Molly and Maggie. Both loved being part of a Razorback baseball family and attended all the Hog's baseball games. Also, they both served as Arkansas Diamond Dolls during their college years.

Also, Molly and her husband, Kaleb, who is a great Christian husband, father, and provider for his family, have given me three of the greatest joys found in Melinda's and my life - three grandsons, Bryant, Briggs, and Brooks Allen.

STORY FIFTEEN: MOMMY-IN-LAW

My mother-in-law, Ruth Stephens, would often spend weekends with us driving up from Van Buren. One time, back in 2013, she was staying at our house and I was spending Thanksgiving weekend hunting deer with friends in Pine Bluff. I received a frantic phone call from Melinda. Her mom had fallen down some stairs and had cracked a rib and damaged some vertebrae. The ambulance took her to the hospital and from there she was transferred into a rehabilitation facility. We went to check in on her and she looked terrible, like she was going to die. Melinda and I decided to get her discharged from rehab and settle her into our house where she would be provided with proper care and attention. We had a den which we adjusted by removing the sofa and putting a day bed in there for her. Her bedroom was upstairs and there was no way she could climb the steps of the staircase. She had to wear this brace around her body to support her spine and it had to be taken off and placed on her by us since she couldn't manage this alone. I suggested she move in with us since she visited us almost every weekend and came to all the baseball home games. So from 2013 to date, she has lived with us, and she is now 86 years young. She is a blessing to be around and has helped a lot with cooking delicious meals and keeping the house cleaned until she had a couple more bad falls which she has broken several bones. Today, she gets around the house with the help of a walker.

STORY SIXTEEN: HUNTING

My first hunting trip was with coach Norm DeBriyn in 2003 and I remember borrowing a shotgun from Tom Pagnozzi. Tom was our volunteer coach at the time and I didn't own a shotgun. Coach DeBriyn had a former player named Pat Anderson, who was an executive with Simmons Bank. Also, this bank had part ownership of a duck hunting lodge known as Lost Island, in Stuttgart, Arkansas. They would sponsor many hunting trips in a year's time. As it happened, Pat invited Coach DeBriyn, Coach Van Horn, Coach Matt Deggs, and myself to come down for a hunting trip. So we went there in the evening, had dinner, woke up early the next morning to hunt, and then return home. It was my first experience and it was awesome. After only one hunting trip, I was hooked. I met one of my really close friends there too. His name was Mike Lambert. Mike was an Arkansas Razorback Baseball fan and went to Fayetteville for most of the games. Sadly, Mike passed away in the spring of 2022 after contracting Covid. He will be sadly missed by all who knew him. Also, I know each and every day, Mike will be looking down on us from Heaven.

Mike was a big duck hunter and a great guide. He knew we needed his help because none of us knew how to call ducks without scaring them away! So Mike came over and that's where we met and became friends.

It was a funny trip because all eight of us were in this hole of flooded timber and we saw a few birds fly up in the dark sky and all of a sudden we heard like six to seven shots. When Eddie, our guide, enquired who shot, turned out it was Matt. Basically, it was his grandfather's old Belgium Browning Shotgun and he didn't have a plug-in it at all. You are only allowed three shots and he fired like seven which was illegal. Matt saw some birds and just went on unloading his gun. It was quite comical because he didn't hit any ducks and he didn't wait for the guides to call out to "shoot". And when we found out he didn't have a plug-in that old gun, everyone just fell out laughing and gave him a hard time. Mike cut a stick as a plug for his gun in case anyone was to ever check him for not having a proper hunting shotgun. Mike and I started to become friends right there and then. He lived in Pine Bluff. He had a duck camp there and it spread over thousands of acres in Bayou Meta. Whenever I would go hunting, be it deer or duck, I would go with Mike.

He retired from the railroad due to a disability. Also, he lived through Lymphoma and various tests and struggles regarding his health. Also, we made another friend named Wes McNulty. He was a farmer off the Arkansas River around Pine Bluff. When I felt like doing more duck hunting, Mike introduced me to Wes and then our hunting trips would comprise of Mike, Wes, and me. Great times with great friends!

Wes had this really cushy camp cabin with three bedrooms, a kitchen, satellite TV, a bathroom, and a shower. Also, he owned an electric golf cart which we would use to get us to our deer stands, and one time at 9 in the morning, I texted Mike to see if he was ready for breakfast. He was, so I got down out of my stand and went to pick up Mike. He was the camp chef for breakfast. As I walked back to the golf cart, I looked down this long cut-through and saw a big buck about 300 yards away. While I was looking at him through my rifle scope, a doe went running through the cut through about 75 yards in front of me. I figured she was being chased so I readied for it. Sure enough, a couple of minutes later, this big eight-point hits the cut-through, sees me, and stops. He was definitely a shooter. You have to be at least three to four years old before Wes lets you take down a deer. So I am standing there, wide open with no cover and the deer starts walking towards me. I already had my rifle up expecting him to appear, so there was no movement. I let him take a few steps to evaluate him and then shot and dropped him. Now, that's hunting! Sit in a stand all morning with no action at all. Then, by chance, you are out walking out for the morning and a trophy comes right to you. Go figure!

STORY SEVENTEEN: CREEPY HOTEL & SLEEPWALKING JORN

As a player and coach, a lot of my time was spent in hotels. Back in the eighties, when I was with Coach Debriyn, we were conducting satellite camps in several small towns. These towns were so tiny and their hotel standards were quite low. We were staying in one of these motels with two single beds in each room and I was in a room with Coach Debriyn, Suddenly, one night, I was sleepwalking and I was standing up on top of his bed. He felt something in the dark and he started screaming, kicking the covers off which woke me up from my sleepwalk trance and I went like "Whoa!" What in heaven's name am I even doing? I looked around and he was flipping out like what the heck are you doing on my bed? and I am totally lost looking around like what is wrong with me?

Similarly, around the same time, we went to the University of Texas to play and they were the team we hated most of all. They were always a superior team in the Southwest Conference days. I remember rooming together with Coach Dave Van Horn and he told me that randomly in the middle of the night I sat up in bed and bellowed at the top of my lungs, "Let them know we're here!" and laid back down and went right back to sleep. He said that he couldn't really sleep for the rest of the night after that. Gosh, what a wild feeling! By 2003, we would stay in really plush hotels, so I would have my own room and I don't think anyone else caught or heard me being weird in my sleep! LOL! I know the people I had previously were thankful not to have to be my roommate again. Actually, it never did bother me!

STORY NINETEEN: READING AND WINNING:

I usually didn't ever read very much, but beginning in 2004, I started absorbing a lot of books due to my spiritual transformation. I was reading the Bible and doing daily devotionals and lots of journaling about what I had read. It helped me open my heart and realize that everything isn't about me, but also about other people who were around me, such as my spouse, my sweet daughters, my players, my colleagues, my neighbors, and my friends. The realization helped me grow as an individual and I remember asking the Lord to forever keep my love tank overflowing so I would give and share immense love with all those I interacted with. When I turned half a century old, I was reborn because I discovered the Lord. It's not to say that there were never struggles, because struggles are an inevitable part of being human. You just need to learn to overcome those struggles without any bitterness in your heart and give it up to the Lord in prayer. Later on, the Lord would give me opportunities to share these struggles with others as a testimony to Him. I would pray for others to relate to these struggles and that they would accept Jesus as their Lord and Savior

I worked hard as a coach to help develop young men to be good family men, good parents, and someone who knew what it takes to work hard and to compete and sacrifice their efforts in life for others. Also, in the process, always being able to tell the truth up front. This is the true process of a great productive life and what it takes to be a true winner.

Similarly, when it comes to winning, my philosophy is simple, even if you don't make it to the top, as long as you have worked hard and given your all, that's what really matters. How you go about your business in life is what's most important. The true and blessed winners in life always give their lives to Jesus.

Because in any game, there can only be one winner, that doesn't mean the other team isn't worthy. I surely always wanted to develop winners, but winning isn't possible all of the time. It's the process that holds the most weight in life. If you are the type of person who wants to take shortcuts to success, I'm sorry, an extremely successful life is just not for you. Many will say slow and steady wins the race. I say, even if you don't win, as long as you've invested consistent effort along the way, those will point you in the right direction and you will achieve actual wins! The effort, the sweat, the turmoil involved, the mental anguish, giving it your all, that's what makes a winner even if you don't win in so called worldly terms.

In the words of one of the greatest coaches, John Wooden, the label of a winner should only be the icing on the cake of your journey as an athlete, as a parent, a teacher, and as a human. The cake you are building is comprised of your hard work, your competitiveness, your aptitude, your attitude, and your potential and the icing on the cake is simply the reward for all you have put into making the cake. A cake without icing is still a cake, but icing without a cake is worthless. You may possess much potential, but potential without hard work and much effort is mostly worthless.

STORY TWENTY: FAMILY MAN

When I would be on the road, I would always be carrying the weight of responsibility of my family on my shoulders. To take care of a family involves sacrifice, financial responsibility, and a lot of loyalty.

I would always ask my players in quite simple terms, "Do you guys think your father, mother, and siblings enjoy having to sacrifice their comfort and monetary benefits to let you be exactly where you want to be and to be doing exactly what you want to be doing? Do you think it comes easy? I know and your parents know that taking care of your family's safety, their good health, and providing for food to be put on the table isn't easy. You need to be mature, work hard to get a good education, and be able to mature and provide for your own family! I would always try to instill in my players that they could not afford to skip classes because they had their parents paying for it. Because, if they had to pay for it themselves, they would be working their butts off while stuck deep in debt and still not be able to remotely enjoy the cushy lives they had now, because of their parents giving to them helping to make their dreams come true. So I tried to teach them to value and respect their parent's sacrifices and try to be worthy enough to repay them one day. To always remember to verbally thank them for EVERYTHING, for every single thing they have done for you.

I would tell them life with much work and effort will usually produce a good life, but adding a life filled with Jesus, and with Him in control of your life will assure you a GREAT life! Amen and amen!

STORY TWENTY-ONE : MY MIRACLE

I had gone fishing with my neighbor boy and his dad in their canoe. We were fishing at Lake Bentonville. It was quite windy and the canoe, after 30 minutes or so, was out of control and we were no longer able to fish. We decided to pull up to one of the small public docks. My little 10-year-old neighbor boy, who is totally eaten up with fishing, gets out of the canoe to fish off the dock. After a few minutes, I decided to join him. As I stepped onto the dock my leg gave out on me and all my weight came down on my collapsed leg with my foot bent back toward my rear end. The pain was terrible. I thought I blew out every tendon in my knee. Somehow, I was able, with the help of my friend, to get home. Later that evening, I was scheduled to attend a church service. My friend, Ron Harris, was hosting and Melinda and I have been going in support of him. Anyway, at the conclusion of this eventful day, and at a service that night many of the attendees and Ron prayed for my healing. That night around midnight, as I was in bed, I suddenly was freezing to death and I started shaking uncontrollably. Melinda checked my temperature and blood sugar which both were fine. She looked online as to what could be wrong with me. But found nothing. About an hour later, I finally started warming up and had stopped shaking. As I was trying to process this, I involuntarily started giggling uncontrollably out of nowhere. But there was nothing that was funny. Suddenly I needed to go to the bathroom and as I got up out of bed I have NO pain in my knee and I can easily walk with no pain. It was as if nothing had ever happened to my knee. It was truly a miracle and a Holy Spirit meeting for me!

Ron Harris has become a very dear Christian friend. He is truly a man of God who serves Him daily as a pastor, teacher of the Bible, husband, father, and friend.

STORY TWENTY-TWO : 2017 SOUTH KOREA

In the fall of 2016 my friend Trey Hillman, who I coached with back in 1989, called me. He knew I had retired from Arkansas and wanted to know if I still had interest in coaching. He had been the bench coach for the Houston Astros and was offered and had accepted to be the new manager for the SK Wyverns in South Korea. I looked at Melinda and she said "That sounds like fun and a good opportunity". So I accepted the job and it truly was fun and a great opportunity to experience. South Korea was a wonderful country with a respectful culture. Trey is one of the best men of God that I have ever known and my time there was something I will always cherish. You see, along with all the positive experiences I enjoyed there the Lord made my dream come true of coaching in the major leagues, even though it was the Korean version of the major leagues.

The player's travel and living arrangements in the country were all big league. I had been away from home from Jan. 30- Oct 10. I had an opportunity to return for 2018 but declined. It was a tough decision because I truly loved it there but the long season away from home was too much for me and I missed my and grandkids more than I thought I would so I finally decided to stay back in the good ole USA.

It wasn't all fun and games though. It was very challenging for us, especially for Trey as a foreign manager. He was only the second foreign manager in the history of the KBO (Korean Baseball League). But he created a culture of fun and love that led the team to winning the championship the next year. I was so proud of him and the players. He even got me a championship ring that I didn't think I deserved but his comment was "Wouldn't have done this without what you taught the pitcher's last year."

TIMELINE

1954: Born

1960: Khoury League

1968- 1972: High School

1976: Rookie Ball League

1980: First Time in Double-A

1981: Released From Playing

1982: Pitching Coach Lurleen Wallace JC.

1982- 1989: Pitching Coach Arkansas

1989-1992: Yankees Coach

1993-1997: Mets Coach

1997: Fired From Mets

1998-2000: Diamondbacks Coach

1998: Pitching Coach Lethbridge, Ontario, Canada, Pioneer League Short-Season Class A

1999: South Bend, Indiana, Midwest League Class A Pitching Coach

2000: Manager of the Team in South Bend, Indiana

2003: Got Divorced

2005: Met Melinda

2007: Married Melinda

2016: Last Year as Coach

2017: South Korea

2018 - 2022: Part-time scout, Tampa Bay Rays

Hey coach, just heard the news. Thank you for everything you ever taught me and for being hard on me when I needed it. You always were straight up and honest with me. You taught me the real reasons for living and that there's more to life than just baseball. Growing up, and being a good man, learning from my mistakes. I can say thank you enough for showing me the right path and straightening me out when I got off of it. Best wishes and hope all is well. Love you, Coach Jorn!

Chris Oliver
RHP

Hi Coach! This is Dick Sanburn. Congratulations on your well deserved retirement! Thank you for investing in all the kids you did and teaching them not only to be great ballplayers but to be great men. I pray for God's richest blessings on you and your family as you begin the next chapter of your life!

Dad of the Pitcher that I coached
Coach,

Just wanted to congratulate you on a great college career, one of the better Coaches I have ever had. I have much respect for you & the way you go about Coaching. I wish you only the best in your next adventure.

-Danny Hamblin
A former player at AR.

Hey Coach, it's Wills. Heard the news. Just wanted to let you know how much I appreciate everything you did for me. You get older and you start looking back on things, and I realized that I learned a hell of a lot from you about not only the game of baseball but about being a man. Congrats on a great career at Arkansas. Proud to say I played for you.

Matt Willard
Former player Ark

Hey coach just saw the news today. I just wanted to thank you for all that you have done for me. Not only in my three years at Arkansas but the years since. Thank you for all the baseball knowledge but more importantly the life lessons you taught me along the way. You will be sadly missed.

-DJ Baxendale
Former pitcher

Heard about your retirement coach and congrats on a great coaching career. I know I've learned a lot from you during my time at Arkansas and it has definitely influenced my career and my life. Just wanted to say thank you for it all and I enjoyed my time with you!

Austin Kerns

Coach, heard about your retirement. Just wanted to thank you for everything you did for me. Even though it didn't work out for me in Arkansas, the memories I have learned under you are indescribable. Best of luck to you and your future wherever baseball takes you.

-Henry Weiler

Just saw the retirement news. You'll be missed but I was glad to hear that you were able to do what is right for you. Thank you for all that you were able to give, both to me and to others, in shaping not only our baseball skills and knowledge but also the character that we carry with us today. I know that the successes I enjoy now would not have been possible without your shaping and nurturing. I hope that you have great success in whatever it is you decide your next chapter should be.

Scott Limbocker
LHP at AR

Hey Coach Jorn

Heard you recently retired. Just wanted to tell you thanks for everything you have done! I am so glad that I got to play for you. You made me a better person and always expected the best. Thanks!

Randall Fant
LHP at AR

Thanks, Coach, and thank you for all the help along the way as a player and as a person. I feel very fortunate to have had you as a coach and hope all is well with you and your family.

James Teague
RHP Ark

Wanted to say it was a great opportunity to get to play for you! Hope you enjoy the time off and find the next opportunity as well. Let me know if you ever want to duck hunt, you've got an open invite. Thanks for everything. Boyd.

Former pitcher
Boyd Goodner

Hey Coach Jorn, this is Brett Hagedorn. I heard you were retiring from the Razorbacks and wanted to tell you congratulations on an outstanding career - to this point anyway. Getting the chance to play for you was a great opportunity and I enjoyed every day of it. I can't believe it's been that long ago now! Best wishes to you and your family in whatever the future holds.

Former player

EPILOGUE

"You just can't beat the person who won't give up"-
Babe Ruth

I hope you have thoroughly enjoyed reading about my journey, including the ups and downs that I have faced throughout my life. The purpose was to ensure you to understand that life is not always happy, bright, and successful. We often feel dejected in our circumstances and at the way life seems to work out better for people with better contacts, better backgrounds, better relationships, and more money. As they say, fortune favors the brave. I have often found myself wondering, if only I had been born in a more privileged household or gone to a more prestigious Ivy League College, would I ever have achieved a lot of money in my life? In my early life, nothing was more important to me than baseball, but when the Lord touched my life and saved me I truly achieved what I wanted, albeit a bit late, but in God's timing, you are never late, your life is always on time, his timing is perfect.

We are all put here for a purpose, and in this life, mine was baseball, and for teaching young men to become productive God-fearing men. I have learned that even the best DNA cannot get you very far in life unless you have a hunger for success and a life given to serve Jesus Christ.

Yes, you will come across people in your life who will only want to see your success taken away from you, the success you have painstakingly worked for your whole life. Just remember that in life, the fiercer you are about success and achieving your ambitions, even the best people with the best resources will not be able to snatch away your hard work. Because with your belief in Jesus and His power and strength you will shine bright enough for them to be forced to notice your own individual talent. One day, your enemies will even acknowledge their support for you, because God's gifts and talents cannot be bought or sold. And that day my dear friends is when you win over your enemy and that is the day you win, actually hit the home run of a lifetime, well done, which includes an eternal life in Heaven at Jesus's feet!

-Coach Dave Jorn, 2022.

Made in the USA
Coppell, TX
10 July 2022

79778309R00090